The true cheesecake and dessert lover is a connoisseur, unrelenting in his or her quest for perfection. Mother Wonderful will never let you down.

Her rich, luscious step-by-step recipes are easy to prepare. They are ideal for those you love, including yourself.

Enjoy a sweet slice of paradise with

MOTHER WONDERFUL'S CHEESECAKES AND OTHER GOODIES

Bantam Cookbooks
Ask your bookseller for the books you have missed

MOTHER WONDERFUL'S CHEESECAKES AND OTHER GOODIES

by Myra Chanin

BANTAM BOOKS
TORONTO · NEW YORK · LONDON · SYDNEY

MOTHER WONDERFUL'S CHEESECAKES AND OTHER GOODIES
A Bantam Book / June 1982

ISBN 0-553-20288-X

Published simultaneously in the United States and Canada

Bantam Books are published by Bantam Books, Inc. Its trademark,
consisting of the words "Bantam Books" and the portrayal of a
rooster, is Registered in U.S. Patent and Trademark Office and in
other countries. Marca Registrada. Bantam Books, Inc., 666 Fifth
Avenue, New York, New York 10103.

PRINTED IN THE UNITED STATES OF AMERICA

0 9 8 7 6 5 4 3 2 1

For Sylvia Daskell,
the real Mother Wonderful

ACKNOWLEDGMENTS

This book would never have been as delicious without the help of some of the finest and most generous bakers in the world: Cory Roberts, Ula Greenberg, Nancy Holm, Barbara Weisback, Fran Landau, Chip Castillo, Carol Spawn and Libby, the Princess Goldstein.

This book would never have existed were it not for the imagination and taste buds of Sydny Weinberg.

My gratitude also to my husband Alvin who gained 15 pounds tasting the failures, and Tony Gardner for his superb handling of my anxiety attacks.

CONTENTS

A Smattering of Other Cheesecake Recipes   78
*A Note for Those Cooks who are Afraid of
    Separated Eggs*   78

MOTHER WONDERFUL'S CHEESECAKES AND OTHER GOODIES

THE HISTORY OF
MOTHER WONDERFUL

I became a professional baker because I expected to be a grass widow. My husband Alvin, that long-suffering saint, and I were not getting along. After six years of marriage I had changed my perception of myself, and no longer agreed with his view of our relationship—that Alvin was *supermarvey* and I was a lucky woman to have the privilege of waiting on him.

The threat of divorce did not frighten me, but I was unnerved by the specter of having to apply for jobs. The openings that were available to a woman with my meager employment history did not coincide with my fantasies. Philosophically I was suited to become the ruler of the world, but since I am known far and wide for my conciliatory nature, I would have accepted a position as Chairman of the Board of the Chrysler Corporation.

Since I did not take instruction well, I knew I would have to be self-employed. The only skill I possessed was my cooking ability. I rarely baked, because I was terrified of egg whites. I could never determine when they were firm but not stiff, and the complicated machinations required to fold them into batter frightened me so that my hands turned into hooves and my tortes turned into pancakes.

But baking frightened me less than a nine-to-five job. I could bake at home and sell my goodies to restaurants. I had been eating lunch at Philadelphia's Fish Market. It's a gourmet restaurant now, but then it was just a small lunchroom that served 20 guests. I told Neil Stein, the owner, that I could make better cheesecake than the kind he was serving. He told me to go ahead and try. If he agreed with me, he'd buy mine.

I suspected that cheesecake was probably the simplest cake to make. I examined 40 cookbooks and presented Neil with my first concoction. He didn't like it. It was too heavy. I tried again, and *voila*! I was in business.

Philadelphia architect Paul Vinicoff, my muse and luncheon companion, offered invaluable help. He ate sweets until his gums dissolved. He advised me to use lime rather than lemon in my basic flavoring. One day in a fit of pique he named me Mother Wonderful. I made that my trademark, whizzed over to my local printer and ordered thousands of business cards that very day.

My customers' requests for firmer cakes fell on deaf ears. My goodies were fine just the way I baked them— creamy around the edges and slightly runny in the middle. I circumvented my clients' wrath by dazzling them with exotic flavors: Ginger Pear, Mocha Blanca, Honey Fig.

I accepted a few more customers and hired an assistant. Alvin was recruited as a part-time delivery boy. Several mornings each week he strolled toward court, a briefcase under one arm and a stout canvas shopping bag filled with cake boxes gripped in his strong right hand.

Although my business thrived, my bank account shriveled. My optimism constantly overcame my prudence. I acquired expensive professional equipment—a Cuisinart food processor and a Kitchen-Aid mixer. The wire whip on the Kitchen-Aid removed all my former terror of egg whites. As my repertoire expanded so did my waistline. In Mother Wonderful's kitchen batter was wiped from hands by human lips—mine!

I shrugged off clients' bankruptcies. Did I have any alternative? On the lists of creditors Mother Wonderful was usually preceded by First Pennsylvania Bank. But even more distressing than their accounting legerdemain were the insecurities of the restaurateurs. Right after rave reviews of some unusual goodie would encourage me to stock up on an obscure ingredient for which there was no other earthly use (I still have quarts of raspberry flavoring in the basement), the owner's Aunt Minnie would decide that very cake was too rich, and I would be asked to try something new.

How can a cake be too rich? The same way a bride can be too beautiful.

After two years, Mom Wonderful gave up the ghost. I passed my remaining clients onto other underground bakers, and breathed a sigh of relief whenever scouts from the Board of Health walked down the street.

I now pass all my secrets on to you.

Think positive: Don't bake when you're distracted or depressed. The cakes will either be raw or burned. Don't bake when you're feeling guilty, or you'll end up covered from wrist to elbow with Band-Aids.

Follow these recipes exactly: They are simple and all have been tested.

Pardon my redundancies: Many cookbook authors prefer to list general instructions in the front and then refer to appropriate pages in the recipes, but I'm writing for people like myself, with short attention spans. I'd rather repeat an instruction many times than have a cake come out defective because the cook was distracted and didn't remember some very important rule that was mentioned earlier.

Try to buy the brand names I recommend: I know they're usually more expensive, but don't cut corners in the name of economy. Always use the finest, freshest ingredients that money can buy.

Find a source for tub butter: If you're forced to use commercially packaged butter, make sure it hasn't been lying around the supermarket melting and hardening and growing rancid.

Avoid canned pressurized nuts: Look for a small dried fruit and nut emporium that does a huge business or patronize a gourmet shop with an owner who would rather dump than sell any food that isn't top-drawer.

Use only the finest imported chocolate: I use Maillard's Eagle Sweet, or Baker's German Sweet, they are the best. Use only Guittard chocolate chips or make your own chips by chopping or grating squares of fine chocolate in the Cuisinart. Whenever possible use pure extracts rather than artificial extracts. They really taste much better.

Bake with professional pans: Throwaway aluminum containers are a no-no generally as they don't conduct heat properly. If you hate to clean pans, line them with parchment paper, which helps brown baked goods and doesn't end up, as foil can, between your teeth.

Sell your body to buy a Kitchen-Aid mixer and a Cuisinart food processor: There are no bargains in life. You always get what you pay for ... except in some very unusual circumstances, like "Mother Wonderful's Book of Cheesecake & Other Goodies," which is worth its weight in gold, but is yours for a mere pittance.

MOTHER WONDERFUL'S CHEESECAKE RECIPES

BASIC RULES FOR
MY CHEESECAKES

READ BEFORE BAKING

Mother Wonderful cheesecakes are exceptional because of the subtleties of the flavoring. Most of these cheese-cakes are variations on a basic recipe. The following 36 recipes are cheesecakes that I have sold to restaurants through the years.

Overbaked cheesecakes offend Mom Wonderful. The center should be custardy. That's not a problem when you're serving these cakes at home, but when you're bringing one to a friend, shifting the cheesecake from the removable bottom of the springform pan onto a plate can be a bit tricky.

Before starting to bake, remove the metal bottom plate from springform and replace it with a cardboard round of equal size that has been wrapped in heavy duty aluminum foil and lined with the same size round of parchment paper. Insert in springform and use this instead of the metal bottom. After the cheesecake cools, remove the cake and the foil-lined round and carry them to your destination in a box. Baking cheesecakes for traveling on foil-wrapped rounds helps cement friendships, because you don't have to repress your rage when your friends misplace all your metal springform bottoms.

To remove cheesecake from the springform just slide a spatula or a knife around the sides, open lock and lift out. Serve the cake on whatever bottom you bake it. The cheesecakes should *not* be lifted off and removed to another plate. Cheesecakes should always be removed from the refrigerator several hours before serving. They have a more sensuous texture and far more taste when they are not too cold.

Keep the mixer speed on low when adding eggs: If the speed is too high, too much air gets into the batter and produces a cake of inferior consistency.

Do not grease springform pans: The crumb mixture has lots of butter, and the quantities suggested will cover the entire bottom and sides of the pans, unless, of course, your fingers have been in your mouth too often.

Always check your oven temperature to make sure it's what it's supposed to be. Invest in a good oven thermometer. Last year at my birthday party, the temperature in my oven was so crazy that I served half-raw veal pâté en croute to 70 dinner guests. Fortunately they were brainwashed into believing I was a superb cook, and they lapped everything up and were sad that I'd made no seconds.

If ingredients are not at room temperature, add 5 minutes to baking time.

When the cheesecake is baked completely, it should be placed in the refrigerator immediately to prevent the development of fissures and chasms.

Cheesecakes should be baked about 2 days before serving and permitted to mellow in the refrigerator. Serve them at room temperature. Although they taste much better fresh, they can also be stored in the refrigerator uncut and boxed for 7 to 10 days. All but the chocolate ones can be frozen.

Never cover cheesecakes with aluminum foil or Saran Wrap while they are in the refrigerator. Condensation will cause moisture to collect on the topping of the cake. If they are still in the springform pan, cover them with a piece of cardboard. If they are out of the pan, store them in a cardboard cake box.

A HALF-SIZE VERSION OF ANY ONE OF THESE CHEESECAKES CAN BE BAKED IN AN 8-INCH SPRINGFORM PAN by using only a half portion of each ingredient and by baking the filling for 40 minutes. Everything else stays the same.

Wherever I could I listed the brand names I prefer for ingredients. That is so that I will not be falsely accused of keeping secrets that make my cakes better than yours.

DON'T BE AFRAID TO USE YOUR IMAGINATION: If you're strolling through a supermarket and see an ingredient that intrigues you, try it. You may come up with a new cheesecake recipe even better than mine.

BASIC (LIME-ALMOND) CHEESECAKE

Preheat oven to 350°F.

Crust:

    ¼ pound lightly salted butter
    2 cups very finely ground crumbs from
        Nabisco Cinnamon Crisps
    ¼ cup sugar

Melt butter over very low heat. Combine butter with crumbs and sugar in Cuisinart until well blended (or combine in a plastic container with a fork). Press mixture over bottom and up sides of an ungreased 10-inch springform pan. There should be enough to coat the entire pan.

Filling:

2 pounds (4 8-ounce packages) cream cheese
1½ cups sugar
1½ tablespoons fresh lime juice
Pinch of salt
4 large eggs

In mixer combine cream cheese and sugar and beat for 2 minutes, or until soft (the cream cheese need not be at room temperature). Add lime juice, salt and blend thoroughly. The eggs need not be at room temperature either. Add the eggs, one at a time, keeping the mixer on the *lowest speed* in order to prevent too much air from destroying the proper consistency of the batter; mix just until each egg has been incorporated into the batter. Pour filling into the crust and bake in the pre-heated oven for 45 minutes. Remove from oven and let stand on a counter for 10 minutes while you prepare topping *(this is a very essential step)*. If ingredients are not at room temperature, add five minutes to baking time.

Topping:

2 cups sour cream
¼ cup sugar
1 teaspoon Wagner's almond extract

Combine sour cream, sugar and almond extract with a rubber spatula in a plastic bowl. Spread evenly over top of baked filling and return to the 350°F. oven for 10 minutes. Remove from oven and place in refrigerator to cool *immediately.* This prevents cracks from forming in the cake.

TRIPLE CHOCOLATE CHEESECAKE

Preheat oven to 350°F.

Crust:

¼ pound lightly salted butter
2 cups very finely ground crumbs from
    Nabisco Famous Wafers*
¼ cup sugar

Melt butter over very low heat. Combine butter with crumbs and sugar in Cuisinart until well blended (or combine in a plastic container with fork). Press mixture over bottom and up sides of an ungreased 10-inch springform pan. There should be enough to coat the entire pan.

*No other chocolate cookie crumbles with quite the same consistency.

Filling:

2 pounds (4 8-ounce packages) cream cheese
1¼ cups sugar
1 tablespoon Myers's rum
1½ teaspoons Wagner's vanilla extract
3½ ounces Maillard's Eagle sweet chocolate, or
Baker's German sweet chocolate,
melted over simmering water in the top of
a double boiler, in a pan over a *Flame
Tamer* or in a microwave oven.
Pinch of salt
4 large eggs
¼ cup Guittard's chocolate chips, or 2 ounces of
Maillard's Eagle sweet chocolate, or Baker's
German sweet chocolate, chopped in a
Cuisinart into chip-sized bits

In a mixer, combine cream cheese and sugar and beat for 2 minutes, or until soft (the cream cheese need not be at room temperature). Add rum, vanilla, melted chocolate, salt and blend thoroughly. The eggs need not be at room temperature either. Add the eggs, one at a time, keeping the mixer on the *lowest speed* in order to prevent too much air from destroying the proper consistency of the batter; mix just until each egg has been incorporated into the batter. Stir in chocolate bits. Pour filling into the crust and bake in the preheated oven for 40 minutes. Remove from oven and let stand on counter top for 10 minutes while you prepare topping (*this is a very essential step*). If ingredients are not at room temperature, add 5 minutes to baking time.

Topping:

2 cups sour cream
¼ cup sugar
1 teaspoon Wagner's almond extract

Combine sour cream, sugar and almond extract with a rubber spatula in a plastic bowl. Spread evenly over top of baked filling and return to 350°F. oven for 10 minutes. Remove from oven and place in refrigerator to cool *immediately*. This prevents cracks from forming in the cheesecake.

Please note:
This cheesecake does not freeze well.

GINGER PEAR CHEESECAKE

Preheat oven to 350°F.

Crust:

    ¼ pound lightly salted butter
    1 cup very finely ground crumbs from
        Goteborg's Swedish gingersnaps
    1 cup very finely ground crumbs from Nabisco
        'Nilla Wafers
    ¼ cup sugar

Melt butter over very low heat. Combine butter with crumbs and sugar in Cuisinart until well blended (or combine in a plastic container with fork). Press mixture over bottom and up sides of an ungreased 10-inch springform pan. There should be enough to coat the entire pan.

Filling:

2 pounds (4 8-ounce packages) cream cheese
1½ cups sugar
2 dried pears, soaked in 3 tablespoons Martell's
    Cordon Bleu cognac for 2 hours and then
    removed from brandy and cut into slivers
1½ tablespoons of the cognac which the pears
    soaked in
2 chunks of crystallized ginger, cut into very
    thin slices
½ teaspoon Wagner's vanilla extract
Pinch of salt
4 large eggs

In a mixer, combine cream cheese and sugar and beat
for 2 minutes, or until soft (the cream cheese need not
be at room temperature). Add pears, cognac, ginger,
vanilla, salt and blend thoroughly. The eggs need not be
at room temperature either. Add the eggs, one at a
time, keeping the mixer on the *lowest speed* in order to
prevent too much air from destroying the proper consistency of the batter; mix just until each egg has been
incorporated into the batter. Pour filling into the crust
and bake in the preheated oven for 45 minutes. Remove
from oven and let stand on a counter top for 10 minutes while you prepare topping (*this is a very essential
step*). If ingredients are not at room temperature, add 5
minutes to baking time.

Topping:

    2 cups sour cream
    ¼ cup sugar
    ½ teaspoon Cordon Bleu cognac (use any
        left over from soaking pears first)
    ½ teaspoon Wagner's vanilla extract
    3 drops Wagner's ginger extract
    1 chunk of crystallized ginger, sliced into 12
        slivers

Combine sour cream, sugar, cognac and extracts in a plastic bowl with a rubber spatula. Spread evenly over top of baked filling. Arrange slices of ginger vertically, like numbers on a clockface, around the rim of topping. Return to 350°F. oven for 10 minutes. Remove from oven and place in refrigerator *immediately* to prevent cracks from forming.

HONEY FIG CHEESECAKE

Preheat oven to 350°F.

Crust:

    ¼ pound lightly salted butter
    2 cups very finely ground crumbs from
        Nabisco 'Nilla Wafers
    ¼ cup sugar

Melt butter over very low heat. Combine butter with crumbs and sugar in Cuisinart until well blended (or combine in a plastic container with a fork). Press mixture over bottom and up sides of an ungreased 10-inch springform pan. There should be enough to coat the entire pan.

Filling:

2 pounds (4 8-ounce packages) cream cheese
1 cup sugar
1 teaspoon rose petal water
1 teaspoon orange flower water
1 teaspoon lemon juice
¼ cup honey
Pinch of salt
4 figs, cut into thin slivers
4 large eggs

In a mixer combine cream cheese and sugar and beat for 2 minutes, or until soft (the cream cheese need not be at room temperature). Add rose petal water, orange flower water, lemon juice, honey, salt and figs and blend thoroughly. The eggs need not be at room temperature either. Add the eggs, one at a time, keeping the mixer on the *lowest speed* in order to prevent too much air from destroying the proper consistency of the batter; mix just until each egg has been incorporated into the batter. Pour filling into the crust and bake in the preheated oven for 45 minutes. If ingredients are not at room temperature, add 5 minutes to baking time. Remove from oven and let stand on a counter top for *10 minutes* while you prepare topping (*this is a very essential step*).

Topping:

2 cups sour cream
¼ cup sugar
1 teaspoon Wagner's almond extract
2 figs, cut into long thin strips (12 slices)
¼ cup chopped walnuts

Combine sour cream, sugar and almond extract with a rubber spatula in a plastic bowl. Spread evenly over top of baked filling. Arrange fig strips vertically, like the numbers on a clockface, around edge of topping and sprinkle nuts over topping. Return to 350°F. oven for 10 minutes. Remove from oven and place in refrigerator to cool *immediately*. This prevents cracks from forming in the cake.

Optional but sensational:

1 cup honey
1 cup sugar
2 cups water
1 teaspoon lemon juice
1 teaspoon orange flower water
1 teaspoon rose petal water

Combine all the above ingredients in a pan, bring to a boil and then simmer for 20 minutes until the syrup thickens. Place syrup in a container and refrigerate. Whenever you make a Honey Fig Cheesecake dribble 3 tablespoons of the syrup over the top of the cake 2 hours before serving. The remainder can be used on ice cream or fruit.

Note:

You can find rose petal water and orange flower water in gourmet shops and Greek grocery stores. There is no substitute for them. They give the cake its very sensuous flavor.

BANANA DAIQUIRI CHEESECAKE

Preheat oven to 350°F.

Crust:

¼ pound lightly salted butter
2 cups very finely ground crumbs from
    Nabisco 'Nilla Wafers
¼ cup sugar

Melt butter over very low heat. Combine butter with crumbs and sugar in Cuisinart until well blended (or combine in a plastic container with a fork). Press mixture over bottom and up sides of an ungreased 10-inch springform pan. There should be enough to coat the entire pan.

Filling:

2 pounds (4 8-ounce packages) cream cheese
1½ cups sugar
4¾ teaspoons Wagner's natural banana extract
1 teaspoon Myers's rum
1 teaspoon fresh lime juice
½ ripe, almost mushy banana, mashed
Pinch of salt
4 large eggs
1½ ripe bananas, sliced very thin

In a mixer combine cream cheese and sugar and beat for 2 minutes, or until soft (the cream cheese need not be at room temperature). Add banana extract, rum, lime juice, mashed banana and salt and blend thoroughly. The eggs need not be at room temperature either. Add the eggs, one at a time, keeping the mixer on the *lowest speed* in order to prevent too much air from destroying the proper consistency of the batter; mix just until each egg has been incorporated into the batter. Pour ½ of the batter into the crust. Insert the banana slices vertically into the batter. Pour remaining batter on top and bake in the preheated oven for 45 minutes. If ingredients are not at room temperature, add 5 minutes to baking time. Remove from oven and let stand on a counter top for *10 minutes* while you prepare topping (*this is a very essential step*).

Topping:

 2 cups sour cream
 ¼ cup sugar
 1 teaspoon Wagner's coconut extract
 ½ cup grated fresh coconut (see
   Magic Bars for coconut form)

Combine sour cream, sugar and coconut extract with a rubber spatula in a plastic bowl. Spread evenly over top of baked filling. Sprinkle grated coconut on top. Return to 350°F. oven for 10 minutes. Remove from oven and place in refrigerator to cool *immediately*. This prevents cracks from forming in the cake.

PIÑA COLADA CHEESECAKE

Preheat oven to 350°F.

Crust:

¼ pound lightly salted butter
2 cups very finely ground crumbs from
     Nabisco 'Nilla Wafers
¼ cup sugar

Melt butter over very low heat. Combine butter with crumbs and sugar in Cuisinart until well blended (or combine in a plastic container with a fork). Press mixture over bottom and up sides of an ungreased 10-inch springform pan. There should be enough to coat the entire pan.

Filling:

2 pounds (4 8-ounce packages) cream cheese
1½ cups sugar
2 teaspoons pineapple extract
2 round slices of dried pineapple, sliced into thin
     slivers and soaked in
3 tablespoons Myers's dark rum for 1 hour,
     then drained
1 tablespoon of rum in which fruit was
     soaked
Pinch of salt
4 large eggs

In a mixer combine cream cheese and sugar and beat for 2 minutes, or until soft (the cream cheese need not be at room temperature). Add pineapple extract, pineapple slivers and rum and blend thoroughly. The eggs need not be at room temperature either. Add the eggs, one at a time, keeping the mixer on the *lowest speed* in order to prevent too much air from destroying the proper consistency of the batter; mix just until each egg has been incorporated into the batter. Pour filling into the crust and bake in the preheated oven for 45 minutes. If ingredients are not at room temperature, add 5 minutes to baking time. Remove from oven and let stand on a counter top for *10 minutes* while you prepare topping (*this is a very essential step*).

Topping:

    2 cups sour cream
    ¼ cup sugar
    1 teaspoon Wagner's coconut extract
    ½ cup grated fresh coconut (see
        Magic Bars for coconut form)

Combine sour cream, sugar and coconut extract with a rubber spatula in a plastic bowl. Spread evenly over top of baked filling. Sprinkle with grated coconut and return to 350°F. oven for 10 minutes. Remove from oven and place in refrigerator to cool *immediately*. This prevents cracks from forming in the cake.

BUTTERNUT CHEESECAKE

Preheat oven to 350°F.

Crust:

> ¼ pound lightly salted butter
> 2 cups very finely ground crumbs from
>   Nabisco 'Nilla Wafers
> ¼ cup sugar

Melt butter over very low heat. Combine butter with crumbs and sugar in Cuisinart until well blended (or combine in a plastic container with a fork). Press mixture over bottom and up sides of an ungreased 10-inch springform pan. There should be enough to coat the entire pan.

Filling:

> 2 pounds (4 8-ounce packages) cream cheese
> 1¼ cups sugar
> 1½ tablespoons Myers's rum
> 6 ounces Hershey's butterscotch bits, melted
>   over simmering water in a double boiler,
>   in a pan over a *Flame Tamer* or in a
>   microwave oven.
> ½ cup chopped pecans
> Pinch of salt
> 4 large eggs

In a mixer combine cream cheese and sugar and beat for 2 minutes, or until soft (the cream cheese need not be at room temperature). Add rum, butterscotch, pecans, salt and blend thoroughly. The eggs need not be at room temperature either. Add the eggs, one at a time, keeping the mixer on the *lowest speed* in order to prevent too much air from destroying the proper consistency of the batter; mix just until each egg has been incorporated into the batter. Pour filling into crust and bake in the preheated oven for 40 minutes. If ingredients are not at room temperature, add 5 minutes to baking time. Remove from oven and let stand on a counter top for *10 minutes* while you prepare the topping (*this is a very essential step*).

Topping:

2 cups sour cream
¼ cup sugar
1 teaspoon Myers's rum
3 tablespoons chopped pecans

Combine sour cream, sugar and rum with a rubber spatula in a plastic bowl. Spread evenly over top of baked filling. Sprinkle with pecans. Return to 350°F. oven for 10 minutes. Remove from oven and place in the refrigerator to cool *immediately*. This prevents cracks from forming in the cheesecake.

APRICOT ALMOND CHEESECAKE

Preheat oven to 350°F.

Crust:

¼ pound lightly salted butter
2 cups very finely ground crumbs from
    Nabisco 'Nilla Wafers
¼ cup sugar

Melt butter over very low heat. Combine butter with crumbs and sugar in Cuisinart until well blended (or combine in a plastic container with a fork). Press mixture over bottom and up sides of an ungreased 10-inch springform pan. There should be enough to coat the entire pan.

Filling:

2 pounds (4 8-ounce packages) cream cheese
1½ cups sugar
½ teaspoon Wagner's almond extract
1 teaspoon orange extract
1 tablespoon Grand Marnier
Pinch of salt
4 large eggs
½ cup blanched, sliced almonds, lightly toasted
2 glazed apricots, cut in half and sliced

In a mixer combine cream cheese and sugar and beat for 2 minutes, or until soft (the cream cheese need not stand at room temperature). Add the extracts, Grand Marnier and salt and blend thoroughly. The eggs need not be at room temperature either. Add the eggs, one at a time, keeping the mixer on the *lowest speed* in order to prevent too much air from destroying the proper consistency of the batter; mix just until each egg has been incorporated into the batter. Pour ⅓ of the filling into crust. Sprinkle with ½ the almonds. Top with a second layer of ⅓ batter. Insert apricot slices vertically into batter and sprinkle with remaining almonds. Top with remaining batter and bake in the preheated oven for 40 minutes. If ingredients are not at room temperature, add 5 minutes to baking time. Remove from oven and let stand on a counter top for *10 minutes* while you prepare the topping (*this is a very essential step*).

Topping:

  2 cups sour cream
  ¼ cup sugar
  1 teaspoon Wagner's almond extract
  1 honey-glazed apricot, cut into 12 thin slices
  ¼ cup blanched, sliced almonds, lightly
      toasted

Combine sour cream, sugar and extract with a rubber spatula in a plastic bowl. Spread evenly over top of baked filling. Arrange apricot slices vertically, like the numbers on a clockface, around the edge of the topping and sprinkle with almonds. Return to 350°F. oven for 10 minutes. Remove from oven and place in the refrigerator to cool *immediately*. This prevents cracks from forming in the cheesecake.

CHOCOLATE MINT CHEESECAKE

Preheat oven to 350°F.

Crust:

  ¼ pound lightly salted butter
  2 cups very finely ground crumbs from
      Nabisco Famous Wafers*
  ¼ cup sugar

Melt butter over very low heat. Combine butter with crumbs and sugar in Cuisinart until well blended (or combine in a plastic container with a fork). Press mix-

*No other chocolate cookie has quite the same consistency.

ture over bottom and up sides of an ungreased 10-inch springform pan. There should be enough to coat the entire pan.

Filling:

   2 pounds (4 8-ounce packages) cream cheese
   1¼ cups sugar
   1 tablespoon Vandermint liqueur
   1 teaspoon mint extract
   Pinch of salt
   3½ ounces Maillard's Eagle sweet chocolate, or
      Baker's German sweet chocolate, melted
      in a double boiler over boiling water,
      in a pan over a *Flame Tamer* or in a
      microwave oven
   2 ounces chocolate mint soufflé or mint
      flavored dark chocolate, chopped up in the
      Cuisinart until they are the size of
      small chocolate chips
   4 large eggs

In a mixer combine cream cheese and sugar and beat for 2 minutes, or until soft (the cream cheese need not be at room temperature). Add the liqueur, mint extract, salt, melted chocolate and chocolate mint bits and blend thoroughly. The eggs need not be at room temperature either. Add the eggs, one at a time, keeping the mixer on the *lowest speed* in order to prevent too much air from destroying the proper consistency of the batter; mix just until each egg has been incorporated into the batter. Pour filling into crust and bake in the preheated oven for 40 minutes. If ingredients are not at room temperature, add 5 minutes to baking time. Remove from oven and let stand on a counter top for *10 minutes* while you prepare the topping (*this is a very essential step*).

Topping:
>   2 cups sour cream
>   ¼ cup sugar
>   1 teaspoon white crème de menthe

Combine sour cream, sugar and flavoring with a rubber spatula in a plastic bowl. Spread evenly over top of baked filling and return to 350°F. oven for 10 minutes. Remove from oven and place in the refrigerator to cool *immediately*. This prevents cracks from forming in the cheesecake.

Please note:
This cake does not freeze well.

GALLIANO CHEESECAKE

Preheat oven to 350°F.

Crust:
>   ¼ pound lightly salted butter
>   2 cups very finely ground crumbs from
>   Nabisco Arrowroot Biscuits
>   ¼ cup sugar

Melt butter over very low heat. Combine butter with crumbs and sugar in Cuisinart until well blended (or combine in a plastic container with a fork). Press mixture over bottom and up sides of an ungreased 10-inch springform pan. There should be enough to coat the entire pan.

Filling:

2 pounds (4 8-ounce packages) cream cheese
1½ cups sugar
1 tablespoon Galliano
1 teaspoon La Torinese Galliano flavor
1 teaspoon Wagner's orange extract
1 teaspoon Wagner's almond extract
4 drops La Torinese anisette flavor
Pinch of salt
4 large eggs

In a mixer combine cream cheese and sugar and beat for 2 minutes, or until soft (the cream cheese need not be at room temperature). Add Galliano, extracts, flavors, and salt and blend thoroughly. The eggs need not be at room temperature either. Add the eggs, one at a time, keeping the mixer on the *lowest speed* in order to prevent too much air from destroying the proper consistency of the batter; mix just until each egg has been incorporated into the batter. Pour filling into crust and bake in the preheated oven for 45 minutes. If ingredients are not at room temperature, add 5 minutes to baking time. Remove from oven and let stand on a counter top for *10 minutes* while you prepare the topping (*this is a very essential step*).

Topping:

2 cups sour cream
¼ cup sugar
1 teaspoon Wagner's almond extract

Combine sour cream, sugar and extract with a rubber spatula in a plastic bowl. Spread evenly over top of baked filling and return to 350°F. oven for 10 minutes. Remove from oven and place in the refrigerator to cool *immediately*. This prevents cracks from forming in the cheesecake.

Note:
La Torinese flavors are quite unique and can be ordered from

The Spice Corner
904 South 9th Street
Philadelphia, Penna. 19147

MAPLE WALNUT CHEESECAKE

Preheat oven to 350°F.

Crust:

¼ pound lightly salted butter
½ cup finely chopped walnuts
1½ cups very finely ground crumbs from
    Nabisco 'Nilla Wafers
¼ cup sugar

Melt butter over very low heat. Combine butter with crumbs and sugar in Cuisinart until well blended (or combine in a plastic container with a fork). Add walnuts. Press mixture over bottom and up sides of an ungreased 10-inch springform pan. There should be enough to coat the entire pan.

Filling:

    2 pounds (4 8-ounce packages) cream cheese
    1⅓ cups sugar
    1 teaspoon Wagner's maple extract
    1 teaspoon Wagner's vanilla extract
    ¼ cup pure maple sugar (fancy grade)
    Pinch of salt
    ½ cup chopped walnuts
    4 large eggs

In a mixer combine cream cheese and sugar and beat for 2 minutes, or until soft (the cream cheese need not be at room temperature). Add the extracts, maple sugar, salt and walnuts and blend thoroughly. The eggs need not be at room temperature either. Add the eggs, one at a time, keeping the mixer on the *lowest speed* in order to prevent too much air from destroying the proper consistency of the batter; mix just until each egg has been incorporated into the batter. Pour filling into crust and bake in the preheated oven for 40 minutes. If ingredients are not at room temperature, add 5 minutes to baking time. Remove from oven and let stand on a counter top for *10 minutes* while you prepare the topping (*this is a very essential step*).

Topping:

    2 cups sour cream
    ¼ cup sugar
    1 teaspoon Wagner's vanilla extract
    2 tablespoons chopped walnuts

Combine sour cream, sugar and vanilla extract with a rubber spatula in a plastic bowl. Spread evenly over top of baked filling and return to 350°F. oven for 10 minutes. Remove from oven, sprinkle with walnuts and place in the refrigerator to cool *immediately*. This prevents cracks from forming in the cheesecake.

APRICOT STREUSEL CHEESECAKE

Prepare nut mixture:

> 3½ tablespoons sugar
> ¼ cup chopped walnuts
> ½ teaspoon cinnamon

Combine in bowl and set aside.

Preheat oven to 350°F.

Crust:

> ¼ pound lightly salted butter
> 2 cups very finely ground crumbs from Nabisco's
>   Cinnamon Crisps
> ¼ cup sugar

Melt butter over very low heat. Combine butter with crumbs and sugar in Cuisinart until well blended (or combine in a plastic container with a fork). Press mixture over bottom and up sides of an ungreased 10-inch springform pan. There should be enough to coat the entire pan.

Filling:

 2 pounds (4 8-ounce packages) cream cheese
 1 cup sugar
 1 tablespoon Myers's rum
 1½ teaspoons Wagner's vanilla extract
 Pinch of salt
 4 large eggs
 ½ cup apricot preserves
 ¼ teaspoon La Torinese apricot brandy flavor

In a mixer combine cream cheese and sugar and beat for 2 minutes, or until soft (the cream cheese need not be at room temperature). Add rum, vanilla, salt and blend thoroughly. The eggs need not be at room temperature either. Add the eggs, one at a time, keeping the mixer on the *lowest speed* in order to prevent too much air from destroying the proper consistency of the batter; mix just until each egg has been incorporated into the batter. Reserve 1 cup of the batter and blend in the apricot preserves and apricot brandy flavor.

Reserve 2 tablespoons of nut mixture for topping. Pour ⅓ of the remaining batter into crust. Sprinkle with ½ of nut mixture. Spread second layer of batter over nut mixture and sprinkle with rest of nut mixture. Cover with remaining ⅓ of batter. Pour reserved cup of batter into the center of the cake and cut through with a knife to achieve a swirl effect.

Bake in the preheated oven for 1 hour. If ingredients are not at room temperature, add 5 minutes to baking time. Remove from oven and let stand on a counter top for *10 minutes* while you prepare the topping (*this is a very essential step*).

Topping:

  2 cups sour cream
  ¼ cup sugar
  ½ teaspoon Wagner's vanilla extract
  ½ teaspoon Myers's rum
  2 tablespoons reserved nut mixture

Combine sour cream, sugar and vanilla and rum with a rubber spatula in a plastic bowl. Spread evenly over top of baked filling and sprinkle with the 2 remaining tablespoons of nut mixture. Return to 350°F. oven for 10 minutes. Remove from oven and place in the refrigerator to cool *immediately*. This prevents cracks from forming in the cheesecake.

Note:

La Torinese flavors are quite unique and can be ordered from

  The Spice Corner
  904 South 9th Street
  Philadelphia, Penna. 19147

MOCHA CHEESECAKE

Preheat oven to 350°F.

Crust:

    ¼ pound lightly salted butter
    2 cups very finely ground crumbs from
        Nabisco Famous Wafers
    ¼ cup sugar

Melt butter over very low heat. Combine butter with crumbs and sugar in Cuisinart until well blended (or combine in a plastic container with a fork). Press mixture over bottom and up sides of an ungreased 10-inch springform pan. There should be enough to coat the entire pan.

Filling:

    2 pounds (4 8-ounce packages) cream cheese
    1¼ cups sugar
    2 teaspoons Progresso instant espresso, or
        Femina dissolved in 2 tablespoons
        white rum
    4 ounces Maillard's Eagle sweet chocolate, or
        Baker's German sweet chocolate, melted
        over simmering water in the top of a
        double boiler, in a pan over a *Flame Tamer*
        or in a microwave oven
    Pinch of salt
    4 large eggs

In a mixer combine cream cheese and sugar and beat for 2 minutes, or until soft (the cream cheese need not be at room temperature). Add rum with espresso, chocolate, salt and blend thoroughly. The eggs need not be at room temperature either. Add the eggs, one at a time, keeping the mixer on the *lowest speed* in order to prevent too much air from destroying the proper consistency of the batter; mix just until each egg has been incorporated into the batter. Pour filling into crust and bake in the preheated oven for 40 minutes. If ingredients are not at room temperature, add 5 minutes to baking time. Remove from oven and let stand on a counter top for *10 minutes* while you prepare the topping (*this is a very essential step*).

Topping:

    2 cups sour cream
    ¼ cup sugar
    1 teaspoon white rum

Combine sour cream, sugar and rum with a rubber spatula in a plastic bowl. Spread evenly over top of baked filling and return to 350°F. oven for 10 minutes. Remove from oven and place in the refrigerator to cool *immediately*. This prevents cracks from forming in the cheesecake.

MOCHA BLANCA CHEESECAKE

Preheat oven to 350°F.

Crust:

¼ pound lightly salted butter
2 cups very finely ground crumbs from
    Nabisco Famous Wafers
¼ cup sugar

Melt butter over very low heat. Combine butter with crumbs and sugar in Cuisinart until well blended (or combine in a plastic container with a fork). Press mixture over bottom and up sides of an ungreased 10-inch springform pan. There should be enough to coat the entire pan.

Filling:

2 pounds (4 8-ounce packages) cream cheese
1¼ cups sugar
1 tablespoon Martell's Cordon Bleu cognac
1½ teaspoons Tia Maria
3 ounces white chocolate, melted
    over simmering water in the top of a
    double boiler, in a pan over a
    Flame Tamer or in a microwave
    oven
2 teaspoons Progresso or Femina instant
    espresso
Pinch of salt
4 large eggs

In a mixer combine cream cheese and sugar and beat for 2 minutes, or until soft (the cream cheese need not be at room temperature). Add cognac, Tia Maria, chocolate, espresso, salt and blend thoroughly. The eggs need not be at room temperature either. Add the eggs, one at a time, keeping the mixer on the *lowest speed* in order to prevent too much air from destroying the proper consistency of the batter; mix just until each egg has been incorporated into the batter. Fold in grated chocolate. Pour filling into crust and bake in the preheated oven for 45 minutes. If ingredients are not at room temperature, add 5 minutes to baking time. Remove from oven and let stand on a counter top for *10 minutes* while you prepare the topping (*this is a very essential step*).

Topping:

    2 cups sour cream
    ¼ cup sugar
    1 teaspoon Tia Maria

Combine sour cream, sugar and Tia Maria with a rubber spatula in a plastic bowl. Spread evenly over top of baked filling and return to 350°F. oven for 10 minutes. Remove from oven and place in the refrigerator to cool *immediately*. This prevents cracks from forming in the cheesecake.

IRISH COFFEE CHEESECAKE

Preheat oven to 350°F.

Crust:

¼ pound lightly salted butter
½ cup coffee-flavored chocolate, grated
1½ cups very finely ground crumbs from Nabisco Famous Wafers
¼ cup sugar

Melt butter over very low heat. Combine butter with chocolate, crumbs and sugar in Cuisinart until well blended (or combine in a plastic container with a fork). Press mixture over bottom and up sides of an ungreased 10-inch springform pan. There should be enough to coat the entire pan.

Filling:

2 pounds (4 8-ounce packages) cream cheese
1½ cups sugar
2 teaspoons Progresso or Femina instant espresso, dissolved in
1½ tablespoons Irish whiskey
½ teaspoon La Torinese whiskey flavor
Pinch of salt
4 large eggs
¼ cup grated coffee-flavored or mocha-flavored chocolate bar (optional)

In a mixer combine cream cheese and sugar and beat for 2 minutes, or until soft (the cream cheese need not be at room temperature). Add espresso dissolved in whiskey, whiskey flavor, salt and blend thoroughly. The eggs need not be at room temperature either. Add the eggs, one at a time, keeping the mixer on the *lowest speed* in order to prevent too much air from destroying the proper consistency of the batter; mix just until each egg has been incorporated into the batter. Add coffee-flavored chocolate, if desired, and mix slightly to distribute it evenly. Pour filling into crust and bake in the preheated oven for 40 minutes. If ingredients are not at room temperature, add 5 minutes to baking time. Remove from oven and let stand on a counter top for *10 minutes* while you prepare the topping (*this is a very essential step*).

Topping:

2 cups sour cream
¼ cup sugar
1 teaspoon Tia Maria

Combine sour cream, sugar and Tia Maria with a rubber spatula in a plastic bowl. Spread evenly over top of baked filling and return to 350°F. oven for 10 minutes. Remove from oven and place in the refrigerator to cool *immediately*. This prevents cracks from forming in the cheesecake.

Note:

La Torinese flavors are quite unique and can be ordered from

The Spice Corner
904 South 9th Street
Philadelphia, Penna. 19147

PEANUT BUTTER AND JELLY CHEESECAKE

Preheat oven to 350°F.

Crust:

>   ¼ pound lightly salted butter
>   1½ cups very finely ground crumbs from
>   Nabisco 'Nilla Wafers
>   ½ cup finely chopped peanuts
>   ¼ cup sugar

Melt butter over very low heat. Combine butter with crumbs, peanuts and sugar in Cuisinart until well blended (or combine in a plastic container with a fork). Press mixture over bottom and up sides of an ungreased 10-inch springform pan. There should be enough to coat the entire pan.

Filling:

>   2 pounds (4 8-ounce packages) cream cheese
>   1¼ cups sugar
>   1 tablespoon Myers's rum
>   1½ teaspoons Wagner's vanilla extract
>   Pinch of salt
>   4 large eggs
>   ⅓ cup raspberry preserves
>   ¼ cup smooth peanut butter

In a mixer combine cream cheese and sugar and beat for 2 minutes, or until soft (the cream cheese need not be at room temperature). Add rum, vanilla, salt and blend thoroughly. The eggs need not be at room temperature either. Add the eggs, one at a time, keeping the mixer on the *lowest speed* in order to prevent too much air from destroying the proper consistency of the batter; mix just until each egg has been incorporated into the batter. Add raspberry preserves to 1 cup of batter and blend thoroughly with a spatula. Add peanut butter to a second cup of batter and blend thoroughly with a spatula. Pour remaining batter into crust. Pour peanut-flavored batter into center of filling. Pour raspberry-flavored batter in a circle between the crust and the center. Cut through both with a knife to achieve a swirl effect. Bake in the preheated oven for 40 minutes. If ingredients are not at room temperature, add 5 minutes to baking time. Remove from oven and let stand on a counter top for *10 minutes* while you prepare the topping (*this is a very essential step*).

Topping:

    2 cups sour cream
    ¼ cup sugar
    1 teaspoon Myers's rum

Combine sour cream, sugar and rum with a rubber spatula in a plastic bowl. Spread evenly over top of baked filling and return to 350°F. oven for 10 minutes. Remove from oven and place in the refrigerator to cool *immediately*. This prevents cracks from forming in the cheesecake.

RASPBERRY TRIFFLE CHEESECAKE

Preheat oven to 350°F.

Crust:

    ¼ pound lightly salted butter
    2 cups very finely ground ladyfinger crumbs
    ¼ cup sugar

Melt butter over very low heat. Combine butter with crumbs and sugar in Cuisinart until well blended (or combine in a plastic container with a fork). Press mixture over bottom and up sides of an ungreased 10-inch springform pan. There should be enough to coat the entire pan.

Filling:

    2 pounds (4 8-ounce packages) cream cheese
    1 cup sugar
    1 tablespoon triple sec
    1½ teaspoons Wagner's almond extract
    Pinch of salt
    4 large eggs
    ¼ cup blanched, sliced almonds, toasted
    ⅓ cup raspberry preserves
    ½ teaspoon raspberry extract

In a mixer combine cream cheese and sugar and beat for 2 minutes, or until soft (the cream cheese need not be at room temperature). Add triple sec, almond extract, salt and blend thoroughly. The eggs need not be at room temperature either. Add the eggs, one at a time, keeping the mixer on the *lowest speed* in order to prevent too much air from destroying the proper consistency of the batter; mix just until each egg has been incorporated into the batter.

Reserve 1 cup of batter. Add the almonds to the remaining batter, mix for about 5 seconds on low speed and pour into crust. Add raspberry preserves and extract to the reserved cup of batter and blend well with a rubber spatula. Bake in the preheated oven for 1 hour. If ingredients are not at room temperature, add 5 minutes to baking time. Remove from oven and let stand on a counter top for *10 minutes* while you prepare the topping (*this is a very essential step*).

Topping:

2 cups sour cream
¼ cup sugar
1 teaspoon Wagner's almond extract
¼ cup blanched, sliced almonds, toasted

Combine sour cream, sugar and almond extract with a rubber spatula in a plastic bowl. Spread evenly over top of baked filling. Sprinkle almonds on top and return to 350°F. oven for 10 minutes. Remove from oven and place in the refrigerator to cool *immediately*. This prevents cracks from forming in the cheesecake.

CHOCOLATE SWIRL CHEESECAKE

Preheat oven to 350°F.

Crust:

¼ pound lightly salted butter
2 cups very finely ground crumbs from
    Nabisco Famous Wafers
¼ cup sugar

Melt butter over very low heat. Combine butter with crumbs and sugar in Cuisinart until well blended (or combine in a plastic container with a fork). Press mixture over bottom and up sides of an ungreased 10-inch springform pan. There should be enough mixture to coat the entire pan.

Filling:

2 pounds (4 8-ounce packages) cream cheese
1¼ cups sugar
1 tablespoon Myers's rum
1½ teaspoons Wagner's vanilla extract
Pinch of salt
4 large eggs
1½ ounces Maillard's Eagle sweet chocolate, or
    Baker's German sweet chocolate melted in
    double boiler over boiling water in a pan
    over a *Flame Tamer* or in a microwave oven
½ teaspoon Progresso or Femina instant
    espresso

In a mixer combine cream cheese and sugar and beat for 2 minutes, or until soft (the cream cheese need not stand at room temperature). Add rum, vanilla, salt and blend thoroughly. The eggs need not be at room temperature either. Add the eggs, one at a time, keeping the mixer on the *lowest speed* in order to prevent too much air from destroying the proper consistency of the batter; mix just until each egg has been incorporated into the batter.

Reserve 1 cup of batter. Pour the remainder into the crust. Add the chocolate and Café & Chocolate to the reserved cup of batter and blend well with a rubber spatula. Pour chocolate batter into the center of the batter in the springform pan and cut through with a knife to achieve a swirl effect, but with the majority of the chocolate batter remaining in the center. Bake in the preheated oven for 1 hour. If ingredients are not at room temperature, add 5 minutes to baking time. Remove from oven and let stand on a counter top for *10 minutes* while you prepare the topping (*this is a very essential step*).

Topping:

2 cups sour cream
¼ cup sugar
1 teaspoon Wagner's almond extract

Combine sour cream, sugar and almond extract with a rubber spatula in a plastic bowl. Spread evenly over top of baked filling and return to 350°F. oven for 10 minutes. Remove from oven and place in the refrigerator to cool *immediately*. This prevents cracks from forming in the cheesecake.

RUM RAISIN CHEESECAKE

Preheat oven to 350°F.

Crust:

  ¼ pound lightly salted butter
  2 cups very finely ground crumbs from Nabisco
    'Nilla Wafers
  ¼ cup sugar

Melt butter over very low heat. Combine butter with crumbs and sugar in Cuisinart until well blended (or combine in a plastic container with a fork). Press mixture over bottom and up sides of an ungreased 10-inch springform pan. There should be enough to coat the entire pan.

Filling:

  ½ cup golden raisins
  ½ cup dark raisins
  1½ tablespoons Myers's rum
  2 pounds (4 8-ounce packages) cream cheese
  1½ cups sugar
  1 teaspoon Wagner's vanilla extract
  ½ teaspoon La Torinese Jamaica
    rum flavor
  Pinch of salt
  4 large eggs
  1 egg yolk

In a mixer combine cream cheese and sugar and beat for 2 minutes, or until soft (the cream cheese need not be at room temperature). Add rum flavoring, vanilla, salt, and blend thoroughly. The eggs need not be at room temperature either. Add the eggs, one at a time, keeping the mixer on the *lowest speed* in order to prevent too much air from destroying the proper consistency of the batter; mix just until each egg and the yolk has been incorporated into the batter. Mix raisins and rum into batter at lowest speed. Pour filling into crust and bake in the preheated oven for 40 minutes. If ingredients are not at room temperature, add 5 minutes to baking time. Remove from oven and let stand on a counter top for *10 minutes* while you prepare the topping (*this is a very essential step*).

Topping:

    2 cups sour cream
    ¼ cup sugar
    1 teaspoon Myers's rum

Combine sour cream, sugar and rum with a rubber spatula in a plastic bowl. Spread evenly over top of baked filling and return to 350°F. oven for 10 minutes. Remove from oven and place in the refrigerator to cool *immediately*. This prevents cracks from forming in the cake.

JAMOCA CHEESECAKE

Preheat oven to 350°F.

Crust:

    ¼ pound lightly salted butter
    2 cups very finely ground crumbs from
        Nabisco Famous Wafers
    ¼ cup sugar

Melt butter over very low heat. Combine with crumbs and sugar in Cuisinart until well blended (or combine in a plastic container with a fork). Press mixture over bottom and up sides of an ungreased 10-inch springform pan. There should be enough to coat the entire pan.

Filling:

2 pounds (4 8-ounce packages) cream cheese
1½ cups sugar
1 teaspoon Progresso or Femina instant espresso
1½ tablespoons Tia Maria
¼ cup chopped walnuts
¼ cup Maillard's Eagle sweet chocolate, or
    Baker's German sweet chocolate, chopped
    or grated (optional)
Pinch of salt
4 large eggs
1½ ounces Maillard's Eagle sweet chocolate, or
    Baker's German sweet chocolate, melted
    in a double boiler over simmering water, in a
    pan over a *Flame Tamer* or in a microwave
    oven

In a mixer combine cream cheese and sugar and beat for 2 minutes, or until soft (the cream cheese need not be at room temperature). Add espresso, Tia Maria, walnuts, chopped chocolate, if used, and salt and blend thoroughly. The eggs need not be at room temperature either. Add the eggs, one at a time, keeping the mixer on the *lowest speed* in order to prevent too much air from destroying the proper consistency of the batter; mix just until each egg has been incorporated into the batter.

Reserve 1 cup of batter and pour the remainder into the crust. Add melted chocolate to reserved batter. Mix thoroughly with a rubber spatula. Pour into center of batter in pan and cut through with a knife so that a swirl effect is achieved, but with most of the chocolate remaining in the center of the cake. Bake in the preheated oven for 1 hour. If ingredients are not at room temperature, add 5 minutes to baking time. Remove from oven and let stand on a counter top for *10 minutes* while you prepare the topping (*this is a very essential step*).

Topping:

2 cups sour cream
¼ cup sugar
1 teaspoon Tia Maria

Combine sour cream, sugar and Tia Maria with a rubber spatula in a plastic bowl. Spread evenly over top of baked filling and return to 350°F. oven for 10 minutes. Remove from oven and place in the refrigerator to cool *immediately*. This prevents cracks from forming in the cheesecake.

ANISEED CHEESECAKE

Preheat oven to 350°F.

Crust:

¼ pound lightly salted butter
2 cups very finely ground crumbs from
    Nabisco 'Nilla Wafers
¼ cup sugar

Melt butter over very low heat. Combine butter with crumbs and sugar in Cuisinart until well blended (or combine in a plastic container with a fork). Press mixture over bottom and up sides of an ungreased 10-inch springform pan. There should be enough to coat the entire pan.

Filling:

2 pounds (4 8-ounce packages) cream cheese
1½ cups sugar
1 tablespoon Anisette
2 teaspoons anise flavor
¼ cup Baker's poppyseed pastry filling
½ cup pine nuts
Pinch of salt
4 large eggs

In a mixer combine cream cheese and sugar and beat for 2 minutes, or until soft (the cream cheese need not be at room temperature). Add Anisette, anise, poppyseeds, pine nuts, salt and blend thoroughly. The eggs need not be at room temperature either. Add the eggs, one at a time, keeping the mixer on the *lowest speed* in order to prevent too much air from destroying the proper consistency of the batter; mix just until each egg has been incorporated into the batter. Pour filling into crust and bake in the preheated oven for 45 minutes. If ingredients are not at room temperature, add 5 minutes to baking time. Remove from oven and let stand on a counter top for *10 minutes* while you prepare the topping (*this is a very essential step*).

Topping:

2 cups sour cream
¼ cup sugar
½ teaspoon Anisette

Combine sour cream, sugar, and Anisette with a rubber spatula in a plastic bowl. Spread evenly over top of baked filling and return to 350°F. oven for 10 minutes. Remove from oven and place in the refrigerator to cool *immediately*. This prevents cracks from forming in the cheesecake.

CRANBERRY MINT CHEESECAKE

Preheat oven to 350°F.

Crust:

    ¼ pound lightly salted butter
    2 cups very finely ground crumbs from
        Nabisco 'Nilla Wafers
    ¼ cup sugar

Melt butter over very low heat. Combine butter with crumbs and sugar in Cuisinart until well blended (or combine in a plastic container with a fork). Press mixture over bottom and up sides of an ungreased 10-inch springform pan. There should be enough to coat the entire pan.

Filling:

    2 pounds (4 8-ounce packages) cream cheese
    1½ cups sugar
    1½ tablespoons mint extract
    Pinch of salt
    4 large eggs
    2 cups fresh cranberries

In a mixer combine cream cheese and sugar and beat for 2 minutes, or until soft (the cream cheese need not be at room temperature). Add mint extract, salt and blend thoroughly. The eggs need not be at room temperature either. Add the eggs, one at a time, keeping the mixer on the *lowest speed* in order to prevent too much air from destroying the proper consistency of the batter; mix just until each egg has been incorporated into the batter. Fold in cranberries very gently with a rubber spatula, being careful not to break them, and then pour filling into crust and bake in the preheated oven for 40 minutes. If ingredients are not at room temperature, add 5 minutes to baking time. Remove from oven and let stand on a counter top for *10 minutes* while you prepare the topping *(this is a very essential step)*.

Topping:

2 cups sour cream
¼ cup sugar
1 teaspoon white crème de menthe

Combine sour cream, sugar and crème de menthe with a rubber spatula in a plastic bowl. Spread evenly over top of baked filling and return to 350°F. oven for 10 minutes. Remove from oven and place in the refrigerator to cool *immediately*. This prevents cracks from forming in the cheesecake.

WHITE CASSIS CHEESECAKE

Preheat oven to 350°F.

Crust:

¼ pound lightly salted butter
2 cups very finely ground crumbs from
     Nabisco Arrowroot tea biscuits
1 ounce white chocolate, grated
¼ cup sugar

Melt butter over very low heat. Combine butter with white chocolate, crumbs and sugar in Cuisinart until well blended (or combine in a plastic container with a fork). Press mixture over bottom and up sides of an ungreased 10-inch springform pan. There should be enough to coat the entire pan.

Filling:

2 pounds (4 8-ounce packages) cream cheese
1¼ cups sugar
3 tablespoons Cassis
Pinch of salt
4 large eggs
3 ounces white chocolate, shaved or
    sliced very thin

In a mixer combine cream cheese and sugar and beat for 2 minutes, or until soft (the cream cheese need not be at room temperature). Add Cassis and salt and blend thoroughly. The eggs need not be at room temperature either. Add the eggs, one at a time, keeping the mixer on the *lowest speed* in order to prevent too much air from destroying the proper consistency of the batter; mix just until each egg has been incorporated into the batter. Add shaved white chocolate and fold in on lowest speed. Pour into crust and bake in the preheated oven for 40 minutes. If ingredients are not at room temperature, add 5 minutes to baking time. Remove from oven and let stand on a counter top for *10 minutes* while you prepare the topping (*this is a very essential step*).

Topping:

    2 cups sour cream
    ¼ cup sugar
    1 teaspoon Wagner's almond extract
    1 ounce white chocolate, shaved or
        sliced thin

Combine sour cream, sugar and extract with a rubber spatula in a plastic bowl. Spread evenly over top of baked filling and return to 350°F. oven for 10 minutes. Remove from oven and place in the refrigerator to cool *immediately*. This prevents cracks from forming in the cheesecake. Decorate top of cake with shaved white chocolate.

HAZELNUT CHEESECAKE

Preheat oven to 350°F.

Crust:

    ¼ pound lightly salted butter
    1½ cups very finely ground crumbs from
        Nabisco 'Nilla Wafers
    ½ cup ground hazelnuts, toasted*
    ¼ cup sugar

Melt butter over very low heat. Combine butter with crumbs, hazelnuts and sugar in Cuisinart until well blended (or combine in a plastic container with a fork). Press mixture over bottom and up sides of an ungreased 10-inch springform pan. There should be enough to coat the entire pan.

Filling:

2 pounds (4 8-ounce packages) cream cheese
1½ cups sugar
2 tablespoons Frangelico liqueur (Praline
    liqueur may be substituted)
½ cup ground hazelnuts, toasted*
Pinch of salt
4 large eggs

In a mixer combine cream cheese and sugar and beat for 2 minutes, or until soft (the cream cheese need not be at room temperature). Add the liqueur, nuts, salt and blend thoroughly. The eggs need not be at room temperature either. Add the eggs, one at a time, keeping the mixer on the *lowest speed* in order to prevent too much air from destroying the proper consistency of the batter; mix just until each egg has been incorporated into the batter. Pour filling into crust and bake in the preheated oven for 45 minutes. If ingredients are not at room temperature, add 5 minutes to baking time. Remove from oven and let stand on a counter top for *10 minutes* while you prepare the topping (*this is a very essential step*).

Topping:

2 cups sour cream
¼ cup sugar
1 teaspoon Frangelico liqueur (Praline liqueur
    may be substituted)
2 tablespoons ground hazelnuts, toasted*

Combine sour cream, sugar and liqueur with a rubber spatula in a plastic bowl. Spread evenly over top of

*A total of 1 cup plus 2 tablespoons ground, toasted hazelnuts.

baked filling, sprinkle with hazelnuts and return to the 350°F. oven for 10 minutes. Remove from oven and place in the refrigerator to cool *immediately*. This prevents cracks from forming in the cheesecake.

ALMOND JOY CHEESECAKE

Preheat oven to 350°F.

Crust:

¼ pound lightly salted butter
2 cups very finely ground crumbs from
     Nabisco Famous Wafers
¼ cup sugar

Melt butter over very low heat. Combine butter with crumbs and sugar in Cuisinart until well blended (or combine in a plastic container with a fork). Press mixture over bottom and up sides of an ungreased 10-inch springform pan. There should be enough to coat the entire pan.

Filling:

2 pounds (4 8-ounce packages) cream cheese
1½ cups sugar
1 teaspoon La Torinese Amoretto flavor
1 teaspoon Wagner's almond extract
½ cup finely chopped almonds
Pinch of salt
4 large eggs

In a mixer combine cream cheese and sugar and beat for 2 minutes, or until soft (the cream cheese need not

stand at room temperature). Add extract, flavor, salt, ground almonds and blend thoroughly. The eggs need not be at room temperature either. Add the eggs, one at a time, keeping the mixer on the *lowest speed* in order to prevent too much air from destroying the proper consistency of the batter; mix just until each egg has been incorporated into the batter. Pour filling into crust and bake in the preheated oven for 40 minutes. If ingredients are not at room temperature, add 5 minutes to baking time. Remove from oven and let stand on a counter top for *10 minutes* while you prepare the topping (*this is a very essential step*).

Topping:

    2 cups sour cream
    ¼ cup sugar
    1 teaspoon Wagner's coconut extract
    2 tablespoons blanched, sliced almonds,
        toasted
    ½ cup grated fresh coconut (see form
        for coconut in *Magic Bars*)

Combine sour cream, sugar and coconut extract with a rubber spatula in a plastic bowl. Spread evenly over top of baked filling. Sprinkle with almonds and coconut and return to 350°F. oven for 10 minutes. Remove from oven and place in the refrigerator to cool *immediately*. This prevents cracks from forming in the cheesecake.

Note:

La Torinese flavors are quite unique and can be ordered from

    The Spice Corner
    904 South 9th Street
    Philadelphia, Penna. 19147

CHOCOLATE FOUR CHEESECAKE

Preheat oven to 350°F.

Crust:

¼ pound lightly salted butter
2 cups very finely ground crumbs from
    Nabisco 'Nilla Wafers
1 cup very finely ground crumbs from
    Nabisco Famous Wafers
¼ cup sugar

Melt butter over very low heat. Combine butter with crumbs and sugar in Cuisinart until well blended (or combine in a plastic container with a fork). Press mixture over bottom and up sides of an ungreased 10-inch springform pan. There should be enough to coat the entire pan.

Filling:

2 pounds (4 8-ounce packages) cream cheese
1¼ cups sugar
1 tablespoon Grand Marnier
1½ teaspoons Wagner's orange extract
Pinch of salt
4 large eggs
3 ounces white chocolate, melted over
    simmering water in a double boiler in a
    pan on a *Flame Tamer* or in a microwave
    oven
1 ounce orange-flavored chocolate bar,
    grated or chopped
1 ounce Maillard's Eagle sweet chocolate, or
    Baker's sweet chocolate melted

In a mixer combine cream cheese and sugar and beat for 2 minutes, or until soft (the cream cheese need not

stand at room temperature). Add Grand Marnier, orange extract, salt and blend thoroughly. The eggs need not be at room temperature either. Add the eggs, one at a time, keeping the mixer on the *lowest speed* in order to prevent too much air from destroying the proper consistency of the batter; mix just until each egg has been incorporated into the batter.

Reserve 1 cup of batter and set aside. Add melted white chocolate and grated orange-flavored chocolate to remaining batter, mix well on lowest speed of mixer and pour into crust. Add the melted dark chocolate to the reserved batter and blend thoroughly with a rubber spatula. Pour chocolate batter into the center of the batter in the pan. Cut through and around with a knife to achieve a swirl effect, but most of the chocolate mixture should remain in the center of the cake. Bake in the preheated oven for 40 minutes. If ingredients are not at room temperature, add 5 minutes to baking time. Remove from oven and let stand on a counter top for *10 minutes* while you prepare the topping (*this is a very essential step*).

Topping:

    2 cups sour cream
    ¼ cup sugar
    1 teaspoon Grand Marnier

Combine sour cream, sugar and Grand Marnier with a rubber spatula in a plastic bowl. Spread evenly over top of baked filling and return to 350°F. oven for 10 minutes. Remove from oven and place in the refrigerator to cool *immediately*. This prevents cracks from forming in the cheesecake.

SOUTHERN PEACH CHEESECAKE

Preheat oven to 350°F.

Crust:

- ¼ pound lightly salted butter
- 1½ cups very finely ground crumbs from Nabisco 'Nilla Wafers
- ½ cup finely chopped pecans
- ¼ cup sugar

Melt butter over very low heat. Combine butter with crumbs, nuts and sugar in Cuisinart until well blended (or combine in a plastic container with a fork). Press mixture over bottom and up sides of an ungreased 10-inch springform pan. There should be enough to coat the entire pan.

Filling:

- 2 pounds (4 8-ounce packages) cream cheese
- 1 cup sugar
- 1 tablespoon peach extract
- 1½ teaspoons Wagner's vanilla extract
- Pinch of salt
- 4 large eggs
- ½ cup peach preserves
- ½ cup grated fresh coconut (see coconut form in *Magic Bars*)
- ½ cup chopped pecans

In a mixer combine cream cheese and sugar and beat for 2 minutes, or until soft (the cream cheese need not stand at room temperature). Add the extracts, salt and blend thoroughly. The eggs need not be at room temperature either. Add the eggs, one at a time, keeping the mixer on the *lowest speed* in order to prevent too much air from destroying the proper consistency of the batter; mix just until each egg is incorporated in the batter.

Reserve 1 cup of batter and blend in the peach preserves and grated coconut with a rubber spatula. Add the nuts to the batter remaining in the large bowl and pour ½ of this batter into the crust. Spread a layer of peach batter all over it and then cover with the remaining batter. Bake in the preheated oven for 1 hour. If ingredients are not at room temperature, add 5 minutes to baking time. Remove from oven and let stand on a counter top for *10 minutes* while you prepare the topping (*this is a very essential step*).

Topping:

    2 cups sour cream
    ¼ cup sugar
    1 teaspoon Wagner's almond extract
    2 tablespoons chopped pecans

Combine sour cream, sugar and almond extract with a rubber spatula in a plastic bowl. Spread evenly over top of baked filling. Sprinkle with chopped pecans and return to 350°F. oven for 10 minutes. Remove from oven and place in the refrigerator to cool *immediately*. This prevents cracks from forming in the cheesecake.

MUNICH CHEESECAKE

Preheat oven to 350°F. Grease a 10-inch springform pan.

Filling:

   3 pounds (6 8-ounce packages) cream cheese
   2 cups sugar
   1 tablespoon lime juice
   1 tablespoon Wagner's orange extract
   Pinch of salt
   6 large eggs

In a mixer combine cream cheese and sugar and beat for 2 minutes, or until soft (the cream cheese need not stand at room temperature). Add lime juice, orange extract, salt and blend thoroughly. The eggs need not be at room temperature either. Add the eggs, one at a time, keeping the mixer on the *lowest speed* in order to prevent too much air from destroying the proper consistency of the batter; mix just until each egg has been incorporated into the batter. Pour filling into greased pan and bake in the preheated oven for 1 hour. If ingredients are not at room temperature, add 5 minutes to baking time. Remove from oven and let stand on counter top for *10 minutes* while you prepare the topping (*this is a very essential step*).

Topping:

    1 cup chopped walnuts
    ¼ cup flour
    ¼ cup butter, softened
    ½ teaspoon cinnamon
    ½ cup brown sugar
    ½ cup white raisins

Combine walnuts, flour, butter, cinnamon and sugar in
Cuisinart until well blended. Mix in raisins with a spoon.
Coat baked cheesecake with topping and return to 350°F.
oven for 10 minutes. Place in refrigerator *immediately*.
This prevents cracks from forming in the cheesecake.
Turn over when removing from springform pan, right
before serving, so that the topping is on the bottom.

ZABAGLIONE CHEESECAKE

Preheat oven to 350°F.

Crust:

    ¼ pound lightly salted butter
    2 cups very finely ground crumbs from Biscuiti
       Vino
    ¼ cup sugar

Melt butter over very low heat. Combine butter with
crumbs and sugar in Cuisinart until well blended (or
combine in a plastic container with a fork). Press mixture over bottom and up sides of an ungreased 10-inch
springform pan. There should be enough to coat the
entire pan.

Filling:

2 pounds (4 8-ounce packages) cream cheese
1½ cups sugar
1 tablespoon Vov liqueur
½ teaspoon brandy extract
1 teaspoon Florio sweet marsala
Pinch of salt
1 egg yolk
4 large eggs

In a mixer combine cream cheese and sugar and beat for 2 minutes, or until soft (the cream cheese need not be at room temperature). Add liqueur, brandy extract, marsala, salt and blend thoroughly. The eggs need not be at room temperature either. Add the yolk first and then the eggs, one at a time, keeping the mixer on the *lowest speed* in order to prevent too much air from destroying the proper consistency of the batter; mix just until each egg has been incorporated into the batter. Pour filling into crust and bake in the preheated oven for 40 minutes. If ingredients are not at room temperature, add 5 minutes to baking time. Remove from oven and let stand on a counter top for *10 minutes* while you prepare the topping (*this is a very essential step*).

Topping:

2 cups sour cream
¼ cup sugar
1 teaspoon Vov liqueur*

Combine sour cream, sugar and liqueur with a rubber spatula in a plastic bowl. Spread evenly over top of

*If Vov is not available, substitute sweet marsala

baked filling and return to 350°F. oven for 10 minutes. Remove from oven and place in the refrigerator to cool *immediately*. This prevents cracks from forming in the cheesecake.

AMORETTO CHEESECAKE

Preheat oven to 350°F.

Crust:

¼ pound lightly salted butter
2 cups very finely ground crumbs from
    Amoretta biscuits
¼ cup sugar

Melt butter over very low heat. Combine butter with crumbs and sugar in Cuisinart until well blended (or combine in a plastic container with a fork). Press mixture over bottom and up sides of an ungreased 10-inch springform pan. There should be enough to coat the entire pan.

Filling:

2 pounds (4 8-ounce packages) cream cheese
1½ cups sugar
1 tablespoon Amoretto liqueur
1 teaspoon Wagner's vanilla extract
1 teaspoon Wagner's almond extract
Pinch of salt
4 large eggs

In a mixer combine cream cheese and sugar and beat for 2 minutes, or until soft (the cream cheese need not

stand at room temperature). Add liqueur, extracts, salt and blend thoroughly. The eggs need not be at room temperature either. Add the eggs, one at a time, keeping the mixer on the *lowest speed* in order to prevent too much air from destroying the proper consistency of the batter; mix just until each egg has been incorporated into the batter. Pour filling into crust and bake in the preheated oven for 40 minutes. If ingredients are not at room temperature, add 5 minutes to baking time. Remove from oven and let stand on a counter top for *10 minutes* while you prepare the topping (*this is a very essential step*).

Topping:

    2 cups sour cream
    ¼ cup sugar
    1 teaspoon Wagner's almond extract
    ½ cup blanched, sliced almonds, toasted

Combine sour cream, sugar and almond extract with a rubber spatula in a plastic bowl. Spread evenly over top of baked filling, sprinkle with almonds and return to 350°F. oven for 10 minutes. Remove from oven and place in the refrigerator to cool *immediately*. This prevents cracks from forming in the cheesecake.

PRALINE CHEESECAKE

Preheat oven to 350°F.

Crust:

¼ pound lightly salted butter
1 cup very finely ground crumbs from
    Nabisco 'Nilla Wafers
1 cup finely chopped pecans
2 tablespoons white sugar
2 tablespoons brown sugar

Melt butter over very low heat. Combine butter with crumbs, nuts and sugar in Cuisinart until well blended (or combine in a plastic container with a fork). Press mixture over bottom and up sides of an ungreased 10-inch springform pan. There should be enough to coat the entire pan.

Filling:

2 pounds (4 8-ounce packages) cream cheese
¾ cup white sugar
¾ cup brown sugar
3 tablespoons praline liqueur or rum
½ cup chopped pecans or cashew brittle
Pinch of salt
4 large eggs

In a mixer combine cream cheese and sugar and beat for 2 minutes, or until soft (the cream cheese need not stand at room temperature). Add praline liqueur, brittle, salt and blend thoroughly. The eggs need not be at room temperature either. Add the eggs, one at a time, keeping the mixer on the *lowest speed* in order to prevent too much air from destroying the proper consistency of the batter; mix just until each egg has been incorporated into the batter. Pour filling into crust and bake in the preheated oven for 40 minutes. If ingredients are not at room temperature, add 5 minutes to baking time. Remove from oven and let stand on a counter top for *10 minutes* while you prepare the topping (*this is a very essential step*).

Topping:

    2 cups sour cream
    ¼ cup brown sugar
    1 teaspoon praline liqueur or rum
    ½ teaspoon maple sugar

Combine sour cream, sugar, rum or praline liqueur and maple sugar with a rubber spatula in a plastic bowl. Spread evenly over top of baked filling and return to 350°F. oven for 10 minutes. Remove from oven and place in the refrigerator to cool *immediately*. This prevents cracks from forming in the cheesecake.

SOUTHERN COFFEE CHEESECAKE

Preheat oven to 350°F.

Crust:

    ¼ pound lightly salted butter
    2 cups very finely ground crumbs from
        Nabisco Famous Wafers
    ¼ cup sugar

Melt butter over very low heat. Combine butter with crumbs and sugar in Cuisinart until well blended (or combine in a plastic container with a fork). Press mixture over bottom and up sides of an ungreased 10-inch springform pan. There should be enough to coat the entire pan.

Filling:

    2 pounds (4 8-ounce packages) cream cheese
    1½ cups sugar
    1 teaspoon Progresso or Femina instant
        espresso
    ½ cup chopped pecans
    1½ tablespoons Kahlua
    Pinch of salt
    4 large eggs
    2 ounces white chocolate, melted in a
        double boiler over simmering water, in
        a pan over a *Flame Tamer* or in a
        microwave oven

In a mixer combine cream cheese and sugar and beat for 2 minutes, or until soft (the cream cheese need not stand at room temperature). Add the espresso, pecans, Kahlua, salt and blend thoroughly. The eggs need not be at room temperature either. Add the eggs, one at a time, keeping the mixer on the *lowest speed* in order to prevent too much air from destroying the proper consistency of the batter; mix just until each egg has been incorporated into the batter.

Reserve 1 cup of batter. Add chocolate to reserved cup and blend thoroughly. Pour ½ the remaining batter into the crust. Spread chocolate batter over it in a layer. Cover with remaining batter and bake in the preheated oven for 45 minutes. If ingredients are not at room temperature, add 5 minutes to baking time. Remove from oven and let stand on counter top for *10 minutes* while you prepare the topping (*this is a very essential step*).

Topping:

>   2 cups sour cream
>   ¼ cup sugar
>   1 teaspoon Kahlua

Combine sour cream, sugar and Kahlua with a rubber spatula in a plastic bowl. Spread evenly over top of baked filling and return to 350°F. oven for 10 minutes. Remove from oven and place in the refrigerator to cool *immediately*. This prevents cracks from forming in the cheesecake.

MARRON CHEESECAKE

Preheat oven to 350°F.

Crust:

>   ¼ pound lightly salted butter
>   2 cups very finely ground crumbs from
>   Goteburg's Swedish gingersnaps
>   ¼ cup sugar

Melt butter over very low heat. Combine butter with crumbs and sugar in Cuisinart until well blended (or combine in a plastic container with a fork). Press mixture over bottom and up sides of an ungreased 10-inch springform pan. There should be enough to coat the entire pan.

Filling:

2 pounds (4 8-ounce packages) cream cheese
1½ cups sugar
½ cup unsweetened chestnut purée
1½ tablespoons Drambuie
1 ounce candied ginger, slivered
Pinch of salt
4 large eggs

In a mixer combine cream cheese and sugar and beat for 2 minutes, or until soft (the cream cheese need not be at room temperature). Add chestnut purée, Drambuie, ginger, salt and blend thoroughly. The eggs need not be at room temperature either. Add the eggs, one at a time, keeping the mixer on the *lowest speed* in order to prevent too much air from destroying the proper consistency of the batter; mix just until each egg has been incorporated into the batter. Pour filling into crust and bake in the preheated oven for 45 minutes. If ingredients are not at room temperature, add 5 minutes to baking time. Remove from oven and let stand on a counter top for *10 minutes* while you prepare the topping (*this is a very essential step*).

Topping:

2 cups sour cream
¼ cup sugar
1 teaspoon Drambuie
5 drops of Wagner's ginger extract

Combine sour cream, sugar, Drambuie and ginger extract with a rubber spatula in a plastic bowl. Spread evenly over top of baked filling and return to 350°F. oven for 10 minutes. Remove from oven and place in the refrigerator to cool *immediately.* This prevents cracks from forming in the cheesecake.

MINCEMEAT CHEESECAKE

Preheat oven to 350°F.

Crust:

- ¼ pound lightly salted butter
- 2 cups very finely ground crumbs from Goteburg's Swedish gingersnaps
- ¼ cup sugar

Melt butter over very low heat. Combine butter with crumbs and sugar in Cuisinart until well blended (or combine in a plastic container with fork). Press mixture over bottom and up sides of an ungreased 10-inch springform pan. There should be enough to coat the entire pan.

Filling:

- 2 pounds (4 8-ounce packages) cream cheese
- 1¼ cups sugar
- 1½ tablespoons Martell's Cordon Bleu cognac
- ½ cup fresh mincemeat (available in specialty stores)
- Pinch of salt
- 4 large eggs

In a mixer combine cream cheese and sugar and beat for 2 minutes, or until soft (the cream cheese need not stand at room temperature). Add cognac, mincemeat, salt and blend thoroughly. The eggs need not be at room temperature either. Add the eggs, one at a time, keeping the mixer on the *lowest speed* in order to prevent too much air from destroying the proper consistency of the batter; mix just until each egg has been incorporated into the batter. With beater on lowest speed add mincemeat until it swirls into batter. Pour into crust and bake in the preheated oven for 40 minutes. If ingredients are not at room temperature, add 5 minutes to baking time. Remove from oven and let stand on a counter top for *10 minutes* while you prepare the topping (*this is a very essential step*).

Topping:

2 cups sour cream
¼ cup sugar
1 teaspoon Martell's Cordon Bleu cognac

Combine sour cream, sugar and cognac with a rubber spatula in a plastic bowl. Spread evenly over top of baked filling and return to 350°F. oven for 10 minutes. Remove from oven and place in the refrigerator to cool *immediately*. This prevents cracks from forming in the cheesecake.

NUT SUNDAE CHEESECAKE

Preheat oven to 350°F.

Crust:

    ¼ pound lightly salted butter
    2 cups very finely ground crumbs from
        Nabisco 'Nilla Wafers
    ¼ cup sugar

Melt butter over very low heat. Combine butter with crumbs and sugar in Cuisinart until well blended (or combine in a plastic container with fork). Press mixture over bottom and up sides of an ungreased 10-inch springform pan. There should be enough to coat the entire pan.

Filling:

    1½ pounds (3 8-ounce packages) cream cheese
    1½ cups sugar
    1 cup smooth peanut butter
    1 teaspoon vanilla
    1½ tablespoons Myers's rum
    Pinch of salt
    2–4 tablespoons Nutella or Chocolate Fudge
        topping

In a mixer combine cream cheese and sugar and beat for 2 minutes, or until soft (the cream cheese need not stand at room temperature). Add peanut butter, vanilla, rum, salt and blend thoroughly. The eggs need not be at room temperature either. Add the eggs, one at a time, keeping the mixer on the *lowest speed* in order to prevent too much air from destroying the proper consistency of the batter; mix just until each egg has been incorporated into the batter. Pour filling into crust. Warm bottle of Nutella or Chocolate Fudge under hot running water, and dribble 2–4 tablespoons of topping over the top of the filling. Cut into the batter with a knife. Bake in the preheated oven for 45 minutes. If ingredients are not at room temperature, add 5 minutes to baking time. Remove from oven and let stand on counter top for *10 minutes* while you prepare the topping (*this is a very essential step*).

Topping:

  2 cups sour cream
  ¼ cup sugar
  1 teaspoon Wagner's vanilla extract
  1 tablespoon Nutella or Chocolate Fudge
      topping

Combine sour cream, sugar and vanilla with a rubber spatula in a plastic bowl. Spread evenly over top of baked filling. Dribble chocolate decoratively on top. Return to 350° F. oven for 10 minutes. Remove from oven and place in refrigerator to cool *immediately*. This prevents cracks from forming in the cake.

MIDDLE-EASTERN CHEESECAKE

Preheat oven to 350°F.

Crust:

   ¼ pound lightly salted butter
   2 cups very finely ground crumbs from
       Nabisco 'Nilla Wafers
   ¼ cup sugar

Melt butter over very low heat. Combine butter with crumbs
and sugar in Cuisinart until well blended (or combine in
a plastic container with fork). Press mixture over bottom
and up sides of an ungreased 10-inch springform pan.
There should be enough to coat the entire pan.

Filling:

   2 pounds (4 8-ounce packages) cream cheese
   1⅓ cups sugar
   1 tablespoon cream sherry
   1½ teaspoons sherry extract
   Pinch of salt
   4 large eggs
   6 ounces of marble Halvah, cut into
       ¼ inch cubes

In a mixer combine cream cheese and sugar and beat
for 2 minutes, or until soft (the cream cheese need not
stand at room temperature). Add sherry, sherry extract,
salt and blend thoroughly. The eggs need not be at room
temperature either. Add the eggs, one at a time, keeping
the mixer on the *lowest speed* in order to prevent too
much air from destroying the proper consistency of the
batter; mix just until each egg has been incorporated
into the batter. Fold in Halvah. Pour filling into the crust

and bake in the preheated oven for 40 minutes. If the ingredients are not at room temperature, add 5 minutes to baking time. Remove from oven and let stand on a counter top for *10 minutes* while you prepare the topping (*this is a very essential step*).

Topping:

   2 cups sour cream
   ¼ cup sugar
   1 teaspoon cream sherry

Combine sour cream, sugar and sherry with a rubber spatula in a plastic bowl. Spread evenly over top of baked filling. Return to 350° F. oven for 10 minutes. Remove from oven and place in refrigerator to cool *immediately*. This prevents cracks from forming in the cake.

A
SMATTERING
OF OTHER
CHEESECAKE
RECIPES

These are cheesecakes that I've also enjoyed or perhaps tasted at a friend's house, found excellent and asked for the recipe.

A NOTE FOR THOSE COOKS WHO ARE AFRAID OF SEPARATED EGGS.

1. Separate the eggs when they are cold.
2. Put the egg whites in a warmed mixing bowl.
3. Attach the wire whip to the Kitchen Aid Mixmaster and begin to beat the eggs on a low speed.
4. When they become frothy, add ⅛ teaspoon of cream of tartar and continue to beat until they peak. Egg whites traditionally should be whipped in a copper bowl. The cream of

tartar replaces some of the minerals imparted to the egg whites from the copper.
Copper bowls that fit into the Kitchen Aid Mixer are available from

> Atlas Metal Spinning Company
> 185 Beacon St.
> South San Francisco, CA. 94080

Egg whites whip up beautifully in them using just the wire whip.

5. To fold in remaining batter, add batter gradually to the egg whites in the bowl. The wire whip on the lowest speed will blend them in beautifully.

CHEESECAKE ORDINAIRE

Preheat oven to 500°F.

Crust:

2½ cups very finely ground crumbs from Goteburg's Swedish gingersnaps
½ cup finely chopped pecans
⅓ cup sugar
½ cup butter, softened

Combine the crumbs, nuts and sugar in the Cuisinart. Cut the butter into 8 pieces and blend in well. Press the mixture over the bottom and up the sides of a greased and floured 9-inch springform pan. Refrigerate until baking time.

Filling:

2½ pounds (5 8-ounce packages)
   cream cheese, softened at room temperature
   for about 5 hours
1¾ cups sugar
3 tablespoons flour
1½ teaspoons grated lime rind
. 1 teaspoon fresh lime juice
5 large eggs
2 egg yolks
¼ cup heavy cream
1 lime, thinly sliced into semi-circles

In the Cuisinart cream together the cheese and the sugar. Blend in the flour, lime rind and lime juice. Blend for 2 minutes. Blend in the eggs, one at a time, the egg yolks and the cream. Remove the springform pan from the refrigerator and pour the filling into the crust. Bake for 10 minutes at 500°F., then reduce the oven temperature to 250°F. and bake 50 minutes longer. Let the cake cool thoroughly on a rack. Arrange the lime slices around the rim of the top to form a border. Refrigerate for several hours, preferably overnight, before serving.

FRENCH POPPYSEED CHEESECAKE

Preheat oven to 350°F.

Crust:

 2 cups very finely ground zwieback crumbs
 ¼ cup melted butter
 2 tablespoons sugar

Combine crumbs, sugar and butter in a Cuisinart and blend well. Press firmly around bottom and sides of a well-buttered 9-inch springform pan.

Filling:

 1 pound (2 8-ounce packages) cream cheese, softened
 1½ tablespoons fresh lime juice
 1 tablespoon grated lime rind
 ¾ cup sugar
 4 tablespoons flour
 1 teaspoon salt
 1½ tablespoons Baker's poppyseed filling
 4 eggs, separated
 ⅛ teaspoon cream of tartar (if egg whites are not whipped in a copper bowl)
 1 cup heavy cream

In a mixer cream the cream cheese with the lime juice and rind, ½ cup sugar, flour, salt, and poppyseeds. Add egg yolks and beat thoroughly. In a separate bowl with the wire whip attachment beat the egg whites and optional cream of tartar until almost stiff. Gradually add the remaining ¼ cup sugar and beat until stiff and glossy. Fold the meringue into the cheese mixture thoroughly by using the wire whip on the lowest speed. Fold in heavy cream. Pour into prepared crust. Bake in the preheated oven for 1½ hours. Chill the cheesecake before removing it from the pan. Serve chilled, but not ice cold.

CHOCOLATE PECAN CHEESECAKE

Preheat oven to 325°F.

Crust:

- ¾ cup very finely ground crumbs from Nabisco 'Nilla Wafers
- 5 tablespoons melted butter
- 2 tablespoons sugar
- 2 tablespoons grated Maillard's Eagle sweet chocolate, or Baker's German sweet chocolate

Combine all the ingredients in a Cuisinart. Grease only sides of 10-inch springform pan, and then press the mixture firmly into the bottom.

Filling:

3 eggs
1 cup sugar
1½ pounds (3 8-ounce packages) cream
    cheese, at room temperature
12 ounces Maillard's Eagle sweet chocolate, or
    Baker's German sweet chocolate, grated
    in Cuisinart
1 cup sour cream
¾ cup butter
1 teaspoon Wagner's vanilla extract
1 cup coarsely chopped pecans
Whipped cream (optional)

In mixer beat the eggs and sugar until ribbons form when the beater is lifted. In another bowl whip the cream cheese until very soft. Add the egg mixture to the cheese and beat on low speed until well combined. In the top of a double boiler, over boiling water, combine the chocolate, sour cream, butter and vanilla. Cook, stirring, until the chocolate is melted and then blend into the cheese mixture. Fold in the pecans. Pour the batter into the crust and bake in the preheated oven for 2 hours. Cool on a wire rack, then remove from the pan. Refrigerate for 12 hours. Serve with whipped cream.

MARBLE CHEESECAKE

Preheat oven to 400°F.

Crust:

- ¾ cup flour
- 2 tablespoons sugar
- ¼ teaspoon salt
- ¼ cup sweet butter
- 6 ounces Maillard's Eagle sweet chocolate, or
  Baker's German sweet chocolate melted
  and held over simmering water in a
  double boiler, or in a pan over a *Flame
  Tamer,* or in a microwave oven. Use only
  2 tablespoons for crust and hold rest over
  simmering water for filling.

Combine flour, sugar, salt and butter in Cuisinart until
well blended. Add 2 tablespoons chocolate and blend until
chocolate is incorporated. Press mixture into bottom
and up sides of a 10-inch springform pan. Bake at
400°F. for 10 minutes, then remove from oven and
reduce oven temperature to 325°F.

Filling:

   1½ pounds (3 8-ounce packages) cream cheese
   1 cup sugar
   ¼ cup flour
   1 teaspoon Wagner's vanilla extract
   6 eggs, separated
   ⅛ teaspoon cream of tartar (if egg
        whites are not whipped in a copper bowl)
   1 cup sour cream
   1 teaspoon Tia Maria
   Melted chocolate not used in crust

Soften cream cheese in Cuisinart. Add sugar, flour and vanilla, egg yolk and combine well. Blend in sour cream on lowest speed quickly.

In a mixer with wire whip, beat egg whites stiff. Fold in cheese mixture by switching to lowest speed and blending in with wire whip attachment.

Reserve ¼ of the batter. Mix in remaining chocolate and Tia Maria, pour white batter into crust. Pour chocolate batter into center and cut through white to achieve a marble effect. Bake in 325°F. oven for 1 hour. Turn off oven and allow cake to remain in oven for 30 minutes before removing. Refrigerate overnight.

FRENCH LIME CHEESECAKE

Preheat oven to 350°F.

Crust:

    1 box Nabisco Brown Edge wafers, finely
        ground in Cuisinart
    ½ cup lightly salted butter, melted
    ¼ cup sugar

Mix all ingredients together in Cuisinart or in a bowl with a fork. Press mixture over bottom and up sides of a 10-inch springform pan. Put a triple thickness of aluminum foil under and up sides of springform pan because cake is baked in a water-filled outside pan and the aluminum foil will keep the water from getting into the cake.

Filling:

    3 pounds (6 8-ounce packages)
        cream cheese, softened
    2½ cups sugar
    6 eggs
    ½ cup plus 2 tablespoons flour
    1½ cups heavy cream
    1 teaspoon vanilla
    ¼ cup lime juice

Beat cream cheese in mixer. Add all the other ingredients one at a time, keeping mixer on lowest speed and mixing until well blended. Pour into crust. Place springform in a pan which is slightly larger and filled with 1 inch of boiling water. Bake for 1 hour. Then turn off oven and let cake remain in oven for 30 minutes with the oven door closed.

Refrigerate overnight.

CHOCOLATE SIN CHEESECAKE

Preheat oven to 350°F.

Crust:

1 package (8½ ounces) Nabisco Famous
     Wafers finely ground up in Cuisinart
2 tablespoons sugar
⅓ cup melted butter
Pinch salt and cinnamon

Combine crumbs, sugar, butter, salt and cinnamon and mix well. Press mixture firmly into the sides and over bottom of a 10-inch springform pan and chill for 30 minutes.

Filling:

12 ounces Maillard's Eagle sweet chocolate, or
     Baker's German sweet chocolate
1½ pounds (3 8-ounce packages) cream
     cheese, at room temperature
1 cup sugar
3 eggs
2 tablespoons sweet butter, melted
2 cups heavy cream
1 teaspoon vanilla

Break chocolate into squares and melt over simmering water in a double boiler, stirring constantly. Set aside off heat. In a mixer beat cream cheese with sugar until fluffly; add eggs one by one, using the lowest speed of the mixer, just incorporating each egg before adding another. Add melted chocolate, then butter, cream and vanilla and mix until blended on low speed of mixer. Pour into springform pan. Bake 45 minutes until sides are firm. Cool then chill in springform pan overnight.

STARCHY LIME CHEESECAKE

Preheat oven to 275°F. Butter well a 10-inch springform pan and dust with ½ cup finely ground Nabisco 'Nilla Wafer crumbs.

Filling:

1 pound (2 8-ounce packages) cream cheese
4 tablespoons flour
1 tablespoon arrowroot
¾ cup sugar
1 large egg
½ teaspoon salt
½ tablespoon butter
1 tablespoon fresh lime juice
1 teaspoon grated lime rind
6 tablespoons sour cream
1 cup milk
4 egg whites
⅛ teaspoon cream of tartar (if egg
    whites are not whipped in copper bowl)

In a mixer whip cream cheese. Add flour, arrowroot, ½ cup of the sugar, egg, salt, butter, lime juice and rind. Beat on low speed for 2 minutes. Continue beating and add sour cream and milk. In a separate bowl, with wire whip attachment, whip egg whites to a peak. Add the remaining ¼ cup sugar and whip until stiff. Fold in cheese mixture on lowest speed of mixer with wire whip and pour into the springform pan. Bake in the preheated oven for 2 hours. Refrigerate.

Topping:

    2 cups sour cream
    ¼ cup confectioners' sugar
    1 teaspoon Wagner's almond extract

Invert cake. Combine sour cream, sugar and extract. Spread over cheesecake.

ANGELIC CHEESECAKE

Preheat oven to 350°F.

Crust:

    2 tablespoons sweet butter, softened
    ¾ cup finely ground crumbs from Nabisco
        spiced wafers
    2 tablespoons sugar
    6 tablespoons sweet butter, melted

Butter a 10-inch springform pan with the 2 tablespoons soft butter. In Cuisinart combine crumbs, sugar and melted butter. Sprinkle an even layer of the crumb mixture on the bottom and sides of the pan to form a shell. Refrigerate while you make the filling.

Filling:

1½ pounds cream cheese (3 8-ounce packages), softened
1½ cups sugar
6 eggs, separated
⅛ teaspoon cream of tartar (if egg whites are not whipped in copper bowl)
2 cups sour cream
3 tablespoons flour
1½ teaspoons triple sec
½ teaspoon Wagner's vanilla extract
1 tablespoon fresh lime juice
1 tablespoon finely grated lime rind
2 tablespoons confectioners' sugar

Beat the cream cheese in a mixer, then gradually beat in the sugar. Add the egg yolks, one at a time, on a low speed and continue to beat until thoroughly blended. Stir in the sour cream, flour, triple sec, vanilla, lime juice and rind.

With the wire whip of the mixer beat the egg whites and optional cream of tartar until they are stiff. Fold in the cheese mixture with the wire whip on the lowest speed until no streaks of white show.

Pour the filling into the prepared pan, spreading it out evenly with a rubber spatula. Bake in the middle of the preheated oven for 1 hour. Then turn off the oven, and with the oven door open, let the cake rest on the oven shelf for 15 minutes. Remove and cool to room temperature. Refrigerate. Before serving, sprinkle with confectioners' sugar.

PUMPKIN CHEESECAKE

Preheat oven to 350°F.

Crust:

  3 cups finely ground spiced wafer crumbs
  ½ cup confectioners' sugar
  12 tablespoons melted butter

Combine crumbs, sugar and butter in the Cuisinart and then spread on bottom and all the way up the sides of a 10-inch ungreased springform pan.

Filling:

  2½ pounds (5 8-ounce packages) cream
      cheese
  3 eggs
  1½ cups sugar
  1 teaspoon Wagner's vanilla extract
  1 cup canned pumpkin
  ¼ cup Myers's rum
  1½ teaspoons cinnamon
  ¼ teaspoon ground cloves
  ¼ teaspoon ground ginger
  ¼ teaspoon mace

Cream the cheese in a mixer on medium speed. Add eggs, sugar and vanilla and beat until well incorporated. Add pumpkin, rum, and spices, blending thoroughly. Pour into crust and bake in the preheated oven for 1½ hours. Remove from oven. Increase oven temperature to 500°F.

Topping:

    2 cups sour cream
    1 cup brown sugar
    1 teaspoon Wagner's vanilla extract

Combine sour cream, sugar and vanilla and spread on baked filling. When oven reaches 500°F., bake for 10 minutes. Allow to cool and then refrigerate.

NO-BAKE GINGER CHEESECAKE

Crust:

    2 cups finely ground crumbs from Goteburg's
        Swedish gingersnaps
    ¼ cup sugar
    ¼ pound butter

Combine crust ingredients in Cuisinart and blend thoroughly. Line the bottom and halfway up the sides of a 9-inch springform pan.

Filling:

    1 (8-ounce) package cream cheese, at room
        temperature
    1 (14-ounce) can sweetened condensed milk
    ⅓ cup fresh lime juice
    ⅓ cup ginger marmalade
    1 cup sliced fresh fruit (peaches, pineapple or
        nectarines are preferable)

In a mixer, beat the cream cheese until it is light and fluffy. Beat in the condensed milk and then the lime juice. Add the marmalade and stir until well blended. Line the crust with the sliced fruit. Pour the cheese mixture over the fruit and refrigerate for 2 hours, or until the cheesecake mixture is set.

COTTAGE CHEESECAKE

Preheat oven to 350°F.

Crust:

    1½ cups finely ground crumbs from shortbread
        cookies
    ½ cup sweet butter, melted
    ¼ cup finely chopped walnuts

Combine crumbs, butter and walnuts in a Cuisinart and blend thoroughly. Press firmly over the bottom of a buttered 10-inch springform pan.

Filling:

    1 (12-ounce) container cottage cheese
    1 tablespoon lemon juice
    ¼ teaspoon grated lemon rind
    1 egg, beaten
    ½ cup sifted confectioners' sugar
    ⅛ teaspoon Wagner's vanilla extract
    1 teaspoon Wagner's almond extract
    1 cup sour cream
    ¼ cup grated chocolate (optional)

Drain the cottage cheese well and place in Cuisinart. Blend until free of large lumps. In a mixer combine cottage cheese, lemon juice and rind, egg, sugar and extracts. Blend thoroughly. Fold in the sour cream with the wire whip of the mixer on the lowest speed. Pour the cheese mixture evenly over the crust and smooth the top. Bake in the preheated oven for 50 minutes. Cool well then refrigerate overnight. Before serving, sprinkle the top with grated chocolate, if desired. Cake will be thin and flat.

CHEESECAKE FOR 12

Preheat oven to 325°F. Grease a 10-inch springform pan and dust with crumbs.

¼ cup graham cracker crumbs
1 pound fresh ricotta cheese
2 (8-ounce) packages cream cheese, softened
½ cup margarine
1½ cups sugar
4 eggs, slightly beaten
½ cup cornstarch
2 tablespoons lemon juice
1 teaspoon Wagner's vanilla extract
2 cups sour cream

Blend ricotta in Cuisinart and transfer to mixer bowl. Add cream cheese and margarine and beat at high speed until creamy. At high speed, add sugar and eggs. Reduce speed to low, then add cornstarch, lemon juice and vanilla. Blend in sour cream at low speed. Pour into prepared pan. Bake in the preheated oven for 1 hour and 10 minutes. Turn off oven. Let cake sit in oven for 2 hours longer. Remove and cool on wire rack. Refrigerate.

GERMAN CHOCOLATE CHEESECAKE

Preheat oven to 350°F.

Crust:

    1 cup finely ground crumbs from Nabisco
        Chocolate Wafers
    2 tablespoons sugar
    ¼ cup melted butter

Combine crumbs, sugar and butter in the Cuisinart and blend thoroughly. Press on bottom of a 10-inch springform pan and chill.

Filling:

    1½ pounds (3 8-ounce packages) cream cheese,
        softened
    1 cup sugar
    3 eggs
    4 ounces Maillard's Eagle sweet chocolate, or
        Baker's German sweet chocolate, melted in
        a double boiler over simmering water, in a
        pan on a *Flame Tamer*, or in a microwave
        oven
    ½ cup strong black coffee, cooled
    ½ cup sour cream
    ⅛ teaspoon salt
    1 teaspoon vanilla extract
    Unsweetened whipped cream and chocolate curls
        (optional)

Beat cream cheese until light and fluffy. Gradually beat in sugar. Add eggs, one at a time, beating well after each addition. Beat in chocolate, coffee, sour cream, salt and vanilla until smooth. Pour into prepared pan and bake in the preheated oven for 1 hour. Cool on cake rack, then refrigerate. Run spatula around edge of cake to loosen. Remove side of pan and garnish with whipped cream and chocolate curls, if desired.

OLD-FASHIONED CHEESECAKE

Preheat oven to 350°F. Butter and flour 9 × 9 × 2 inch pan.

Filling:

1½ pounds farmer cheese
1 (8-ounce) package cream cheese
1 (12-ounce) container dry cottage cheese, or
    small-curd cottage cheese, drained
1½ cups sugar
1 teaspoon cinnamon
4 large eggs, beaten
1 cup white raisins

Mix cheeses together in Cuisinart until well blended. Add sugar and cinnamon. Blend in eggs. Fold in raisins with a spoon. Reserve.

Dough:

4 cups sifted flour
2 teaspoons baking powder
1½ cups sugar
½ cup salad oil
2 eggs, well beaten
⅓ cup ice water
2 tablespoons sugar mixed with ¼ teaspoon
    cinnamon

Sift flour, baking powder and sugar into Cuisinart. Blend in oil and eggs for 3 seconds. Add water gradually through the feed tube while Cuisinart is running until the dough forms a soft ball. Divide the dough into three pieces, one larger than the other two. Grease and flour a 9 × 9 × 2-inch pan. Roll out the larger piece to a 12½-inch square and line bottom and sides of pan with it. Spread ½ the filling over the dough. Roll out second piece of dough to an 8-inch square. Put in pan over filling. Place remaining filling on top of second layer of dough. Roll out third piece of dough into an 8½-inch square and place over filling. Press edges of bottom and top layers of dough together. Trim off excess. Make 6 slits in top layer of dough. Sprinkle sugar-cinnamon mixture over top. Bake in the preheated oven for 1 hour 10 minutes, or until fork inserted in center of cake comes out clean and top is golden brown. Cool on rack.

PINEAPPLE CHEESECAKE

Preheat oven to 350°F.

16 single Nabisco Cinnamon Crisps,
　　crumbled
1 cup drained, crushed pineapple
1½ pounds (3 8-ounce packages) cream cheese,
　　at room temperature
1 cup sugar
4 eggs
1 teaspoon Wagner's vanilla extract
1 pint sour cream

Sprinkle crumbs on bottom of a 10-inch springform pan, then place pineapple over crumbs. Beat the cream cheese in mixer until smooth. Add sugar gradually, beating constantly. Add the eggs, one at a time, beating well on low speed after each addition. Add the vanilla and sour cream and beat until smooth. Pour over pineapple. Bake in the preheated oven for 1 hour. Cool on a rack. Loosen cake from side of pan with a sharp knife and release. Invert before serving.

RICOTTA CHEESECAKE

Preheat oven to 375°F.

Crust:

    2 cups macaroon crumbs
    4 tablespoons butter, melted
    ¼ cup sugar

Blend the ingredients in Cuisinart. Press crumb mix over bottom and ½ way up sides of a 10-inch springform pan. Refrigerate until filling is prepared.

Filling:

    4 eggs
    1 cup sugar
    1½ pounds fresh ricotta cheese
    ¼ cup walnut pieces
    2 ounces shaved white chocolate
    2 tablespoons chopped candied ginger
    1 tablespoon flour
    1½ teaspoons Myers's rum

In a mixer beat the eggs until they become lemon colored. Gradually add sugar. Mix in ricotta cheese. Combine nuts, chocolate and ginger and dust with flour. Add to batter and blend in. Add rum and mix until well combined. Pour into crust and bake in the preheated oven for 1 hour 15 minutes. Chill.

ANISE PEAR CHEESECAKE

Preheat oven to 400°F.

Crust:

1 cup sifted flour
2 tablespoons sugar
¼ teaspoon salt
½ cup softened butter
1 egg yolk (save egg white for filling)

Combine flour, sugar, salt, butter and egg yolk in Cuisinart until soft dough is formed. Pat out over bottom and up sides of a 9-inch springform pan. Bake for 10 minutes. Remove from oven and reset oven to 350°F.

Pears:

3 fresh Bartlett pears
2 cups water
1 tablespoon lemon juice

Peel, core and cut pears in half lengthwise. Heat water and lemon juice in a large skillet. Place pear halves, cut side down in the water. Cover and cook for 2 minutes. Turn pears over, cover and cook for 1 minute more. Remove pears from liquid and set aside.

Filling:

6 ounces cream cheese
1/3 cup sugar
1 1/2 teaspoons flour
1/4 teaspoon salt
1 teaspoon Wagner's vanilla
1 teaspoon lemon juice
2 large eggs, separated
1/8 teaspoon cream of tartar (if egg whites
     are not whipped in copper bowl)
1 egg white left over from crust
1/2 cup sour cream
3/4 teaspoon ground anise

Soften cream cheese in Cuisinart. Mix sugar, flour and salt together. Add to cream cheese and cut in until blended. Add vanilla, lemon juice and egg yolks and blend until smooth. Blend in sour cream. Beat egg whites with wire whip in mixer until soft peaks form. Fold cheese mixture and 1/2 teaspoon anise into egg whites with wire whip on lowest speed of mixer until completely combined. Turn into prepared crust and arrange poached pear halves, cut side up, on top. Sprinkle with remaining 1/4 teaspoon anise. Bake in preheated oven for 50 minutes. Cool on rack then refrigerate until ready to serve.

CAKES

SOME NOTES ABOUT CAKES

None of the following cakes are layer cakes. Most layer cakes are bland and uninteresting. If they weren't they wouldn't require so much icing to dress them. Only one of these cakes requires icing—Chocolate Crime. Most of these cakes require only a dusting with confectioners' sugar right before serving.

Cakes should cool in the pan, on racks, or elevated on two similarly sized cans, so that air can get around and under them. The most important pan in this section is a 10 × 4-inch tube pan of professional quality, made of very heavy aluminum with a center that does not come out. If the pan is well greased and dusted with flour, there will be no problems in removing the cake.

HOW TO KNOW IF YOUR CAKE IS DONE

1. E.S.P.
2. Insert a cake tester or a knife into the center of the

cake and if it comes out completely clean, the cake is done.

3. Hold the cake up to your ear. If there is any snap, crackle or popping noise, that means the eggs are still combining with the other ingredients. When the cake is silent, it is done.

PINEAPPLE NUT POUND CAKE

¾ cup sugar
3 tablespoons flour
Pinch of salt
¾ cup pineapple juice
3 egg yolks, slightly beaten
2 tablespoons butter
½ cup well-drained pineapple chunks

In the top of a double boiler over simmering water combine sugar, flour and salt. Add pineapple juice and egg yolks. Cook, stirring, until mixture thickens. When thick, add butter and pineapple chunks. Set aside to cool.

2 tablespoons butter, melted
½ cup chopped walnuts
½ cup brown sugar, packed
2 teaspoons cinnamon
2 teaspoons flour

Melt butter, add to nuts and coat well. Add brown sugar, cinnamon and flour. Toss well.

Preheat oven to 350°F. Grease and flour 10 × 4-inch tube pan.

1 cup butter
½ cup vegetable oil
3 cups sugar
6 extra-large eggs
1 cup buttermilk
2 teaspoons Wagner's vanilla extract
1 teaspoon lime juice
3 cups flour
½ teaspoon baking powder
Pinch of salt
Confectioners' sugar

In a mixer beat butter, oil and sugar until fluffy. Add eggs, one at a time, beating well after each addition. Add vanilla and lime juice. Combine flour, baking powder and salt. Add to batter alternately with buttermilk, beginning and ending with the flour (⅓ flour, ½ buttermilk, ⅓ flour, ½ buttermilk, ⅓ flour). Pour into the prepared pan and bake in preheated oven for 30 minutes. Remove from oven and push pineapple and nut mixtures into already partially baked batter carefully. Return to oven and bake for 50 minutes more, or until a knife or tester inserted in the center of the cake comes out clean. Cool on rack. Sprinkle with confectioners' sugar.

GERMAN BUNDT CAKE

Have all ingredients at room temperature for 3 hours before starting cake. Butter well a Bundt pan.

Preheat oven to 350°F.

1 cup sweet butter
1¼ cup granulated sugar
1 cup confectioners' sugar
4 eggs, separated
⅛ teaspoon cream of tartar (if egg whites
    are not whipped in copper bowl)
1 teaspoon Wagner's vanilla extract
1 teaspoon Wagner's almond extract
3 cups cake flour, sifted 3 times
2 teaspoons baking powder
½ teaspoon salt
1 cup milk
¾ cup blanched almonds
Confectioners' sugar

In mixer cream butter. Sift sugars together and gradually add to butter. Add egg yolks, one at a time, and beat until smooth. Mix in extracts. Combine sifted flour, baking powder and salt and sift 3 more times. Add flour mixture and milk alternately to batter, starting and ending with flour (⅓ flour, ½ buttermilk, ⅓ flour, ½ buttermilk, ⅓ flour). Beat egg whites and optional cream of tartar until stiff with wire whip of the mixer. Fold into batter with wire whip attachment on lowest speed. Put large dabs of butter along crease of mold, embedding an almond in each dab of butter. Pour batter into pan. Bake in the preheated oven for 1 hour and 15 minutes or until knife or tester inserted in cake comes out clean. Remove cake from oven and let cool on a rack for 15 minutes before turning out of pan. Sprinkle with confectioners' sugar.

SOUTHERN COCONUT CAKE

Preheat oven to 325°F. Butter or line with parchment paper ONLY the bottom of a 10 × 4-inch tube pan.

½ pound white chocolate, melted over
    simmering water in a double boiler, in a
    pan on a *Flame Tamer*, or in microwave
    oven
1 cup butter
2 cups sugar
4 eggs, separated
⅛ teaspoon cream of tartar (if egg
    whites will not be whipped in a
    copper bowl)
2½ cups flour, sifted
1 teaspoon baking powder
½ teaspoon salt
1 cup skim milk
1 teaspoon lemon juice
1 cup chopped pecans
1 cup grated fresh coconut
1 teaspoon Wagner's vanilla extract

In Cuisinart cream butter and sugar. Add egg yolks and cut in. Add chocolate, vanilla, and cut in. Sift flour, baking powder and salt together. Combine milk and lemon juice. Add flour mixture and milk mixture alternately to chocolate mixture beginning and ending with flour (⅓ flour, ½ milk, ⅓ flour, ½ milk, ⅓ flour). In mixer whip egg whites with optional cream of tartar until stiff with wire whip. Fold in egg whites, pecans and coconut then batter using wire whip on lowest speed of mixer. Bake for 1 hour and 20 minutes. Cool for 30 minutes and then turn out on a rack. If you think you will have trouble getting the cake out of the pan, then grease or line the entire tube pan. The top of this cake tends to crack.

BRANDIED POUND CAKE

Preheat oven to 325°F. Butter and flour a 10 × 4-inch tube pan.

1 pound butter
3 cups sugar
6 extra-large eggs
3 tablespoons cognac
1 teaspoon mace
3½ cups unsifted flour
¾ cup evaporated milk mixed with ¼ cup water
Confectioners' sugar

In a mixer beat the butter and sugar until fluffy and light in color. Add the eggs, one at a time, beating well after each addition. Add cognac and mace. Add flour alternately with milk-water mixture, with flour in three parts and milk-water in two parts (⅓ flour, ½ milk, ⅓ flour, ½ milk, ⅓ flour). Bake in the preheated oven for 2 hours, or until a knife inserted in the center comes out clean. Cool on a rack. Sprinkle with confectioners' sugar.

Note:

This is a very high cake and is best baked the day before serving. It will form a high crown. When unmolding the cake have 2 cake plates ready as the cake should have the crown on top.

SOUR CREAM COFFEE CAKE

Preheat oven to 350°F. Line a 9 × 13-inch pan with buttered parchment paper.

Filling:

- ½ pound sweet butter
- ¾ cup sugar
- 3 large eggs
- 2½ cups sifted flour
- 1 teaspoon baking soda
- 2 teaspoons baking powder
- 1 cup sour cream
- 1 cup apricot preserves

Topping:

- ¾ cup sugar
- 2 teaspoons cinnamon
- 1 cup chopped walnuts (¼ pound)

In mixer, cream butter and sugar. Beat in eggs, one at a time. Combine flour, baking soda and baking powder in a separate bowl. Add to batter in thirds, alternating with sour cream (⅓ flour, ½ sour cream, ⅓ flour, ½ sour cream, ⅓ flour). Blend thoroughly (don't be alarmed if batter is sticky). Spread half the batter over bottom of the prepared pan. Spread preserves over batter. Sprinkle half of nut topping over preserves. Top with rest of batter (drop it in small amounts, using fingers or spatula, or both. It's easier to manipulate that way). Sprinkle with remaining nut topping. Bake in the preheated oven for 50 minutes, or until a knife or tester inserted in the center comes out clean. Cool on rack.

Note:

For more exotic flavors try damson plum preserves and pine nuts or raspberry preserves and blanched sliced almonds or blueberry preserves and pecans.

Do not double this recipe and bake it in a large pan. It comes out overbaked around the sides.

TUTTI-FRUITI CARROT CAKE

Preheat oven to 325°F. Butter and flour 10 × 4-inch tube pan.

1½ cups oil
2 cups sugar
4 eggs
1 teaspoon salt
2 cups flour
2 teaspoons baking soda
1 teaspoon Wagner's cinnamon extract
1½ cups grated carrots (about 1 pound)
½ cup chopped walnuts
½ cup white raisins, soaked in brandy for ½
hour, then carefully drained
½ cup drained crushed pineapple
2 ounces Maillard's Eagle sweet chocolate, or
Baker's German sweet chocolate, grated
Confectioners' sugar

With the mixer's whip attached, cream the oil and sugar. Add the eggs, one at a time, beating well after each addition. Sift together salt, flour and baking soda. Add to batter and blend. Add cinnamon extract, carrots, walnuts, raisins, pineapple and chocolate and blend thoroughly.

Pour batter into pan and bake in the preheated oven for 1½ hours until a knife or tester inserted into the center of the cake comes out clean. Cool on rack. Turn cake upside down into serving plate. Before serving sprinkle with confectioners' sugar.

Optional Icing:

1 (8-ounce package) cream
      cheese, softened
4 tablespoons sweet butter, melted
1 tablespoon lime juice
½ pound confectioners' sugar

Beat cream cheese until light and fluffy. Gradually add the melted butter, beating until it is completely absorbed. Add lime juice, then add sugar gradually, beating well until the icing is smooth. Spread on cake and refrigerate to set.

POPPYSEED POUND CAKE

Preheat oven to 300°F. Grease and flour 10 × 4-inch tube pan.

- 1 cup butter
- 3 cups sugar
- 6 eggs, separated
- ¼ teaspoon baking soda
- 3 cups sifted flour
- 1 cup sour cream
- 1 teaspoon lime juice
- ¼ cup Baker's poppyseed pastry filling
- ½ cup large walnut pieces
- ⅛ teaspoon cream of tartar (if egg whites are not whipped in copper bowl)
- Confectioner's sugar

In mixer cream butter and sugar thoroughly. Stir in egg yolks one at a time. Add soda to flour. Add flour and sour cream to batter alternately beginning and ending with flour (⅓ flour, ½ sour cream, ⅓ flour, ½ sour cream, ⅓ flour). Stir in lime juice, poppyseed and walnuts. Beat egg whites with optional cream of tartar until stiff with wire whip on high speed. Fold in batter with wire whip on lowest speed until completely blended together. Bake for 2 hours and 15 minutes or until knife or tester inserted in center of cake comes out clean. Let cool for 30 minutes before taking out of pan. Cake should be served right side up, sprinkled with confectioners' sugar.

WHITE CHOCOLATE CHIP POUND CAKE

Preheat oven to 325°F. Butter a 10 × 4-inch tube pan.

1 cup sweet butter
1 (8-ounce) package cream cheese
2 cups sugar
1 teaspoon Wagner's coffee extract
2 teaspoons Wagner's vanilla extract
4 large eggs
2 teaspoons baking powder
2 cups sifted flour
6 ounces white chocolate, chopped into
    chip-sized pieces in the Cuisinart
½ cup finely chopped black or English walnuts
Confectioners' sugar

Cream butter, cream cheese and sugar in mixer until fluffy, then add the extracts. Add eggs, one at a time, beating well after each addition. Sift together baking powder and flour. Add to batter and beat at medium to high speed until flour is completely incorporated. By hand stir in chocolate bits. Coat prepared pan with nuts. Do sides of pan first (use your hand if necessary to make nuts adhere to sides), then coat bottom of pan with the remaining nuts. Bake in the preheated oven for 1 hour and 20 minutes, or until a knife or tester inserted in the center comes out clean. Cool on rack. Sprinkle with confectioners' sugar.

SPICE CAKE

Preheat oven to 350°F. Butter and flour 10 × 4-inch tube pan.

  1½ cups sugar
  6 ounces butter
  3 large eggs
  2 cups flour
  1 teaspoon baking powder
  ½ teaspoon baking soda
  2 teaspoons nutmeg
  1 teaspoon cinnamon
  1 teaspoon allspice
  ½ teaspoon salt
  1 cup buttermilk
  ½ cup coarsely chopped pecans
  Confectioners' sugar

In mixer cream butter and sugar. Add eggs, one at a time, beating well after each addition. Sift together flour, baking powder, soda, spices and salt. Mix flour mixture into batter in three parts, alternating with buttermilk (⅓ flour, ½ buttermilk, ⅓ flour, ½ buttermilk, ⅓ flour). Add nuts. Bake in a greased and floured 10-inch tube pan for 55 minutes, or until knife or tester inserted in cake comes out clean. Cool on a rack. Sprinkle with confectioners' sugar.

CONFECTIONERS' SUGAR POUND CAKE

Preheat oven to 350°F. Butter and flour 10 × 4-inch tube pan.

- ¾ pound butter, at room temperature
- 1 pound confectioners' sugar, sifted
- 1 tablespoon brandy
- 1 teaspoon mace
- 6 large eggs
- 2½ cups flour
- Confectioners' sugar

Beat butter until fluffy. Add sugar, then brandy and mace. Beat in eggs, one at a time, at high speed. Add flour and mix well. Bake in the preheated oven for 1 hour and 5 minutes or until a knife or tester inserted in the center comes out clean. Cool on rack. Sprinkle with confectioners' sugar.

Note:

Best if baked 2 to 3 days before eating. It should season wrapped in plastic wrap.

CHOCOLATE CRIME

Preheat oven to 350°F. Butter 13 × 9 × 2-inch pan.

- 1 cup half-and-half
- 1 teaspoon raspberry vinegar
- 1 teaspoon baking soda
- 1 teaspoon Kahlua
- 1 cup hot water
- 8 ounces butter, melted
- ¼ cup cocoa
- 2 cups sugar
- 2 large eggs
- 2 cups flour
- 1 teaspoon Progresso or Femina instant espresso

This cake may be mixed with a spoon or a whisk. Combine half-and-half, vinegar, baking soda and Kahlua in a bowl and set aside. In a bowl blend the water, butter and cocoa. Add sugar, then eggs. Combine flour and espresso. Mix flour and half-and-half mixture alternately into batter (⅓ flour, ½ half and half, ⅓ flour, ½ half and half, ⅓ flour). Don't be afraid if batter seems thin and runny. It should be that way. Bake 45 minutes. Cool on rack.

This is best with icing:

- ½ cup half-and-half
- 1 teaspoon Progresso or Femina instant espresso
- 6 tablespoons butter
- 1 cup sugar
- 8 ounces Maillard's Eagle sweet chocolate, or Baker's German sweet chocolate, in chip-sized pieces

In a pot, scald half-and-half and espresso. Then add all at once butter, sugar and chips. Bring to a boil. Pour over hot cake.

GINGER CAKE

Preheat oven to 350°F. Butter and flour 10 × 4-inch tube pan.

½ cup preserved ginger, chopped in Cuisinart
¼ cup brandy
2 cups flour
½ pound butter
1 cup sugar
6 eggs
2 teaspoons ground ginger
½ cup chopped walnuts
Confectioners' sugar

Soak preserved ginger in brandy overnight, then drain. Add ½ cup of the flour to the ginger and stir well. To the brandy remaining, add enough additional brandy to equal ¼ cup. Beat butter until fluffy. Add sugar and beat until well combined. Add eggs, one at a time, beating well after each addition. Mix the remaining 1½ cups flour with ground ginger. Mix flour into cake. Add brandy, nuts and the preserved ginger. Mix until well distributed. Bake for 60 minutes or until cake tests done. Cool on rack. This cake does not rise a great deal. It is dense. It should be thinly sliced. Sprinkle with confectioners' sugar.

CRANBERRY NUT TORTE

Preheat oven to 350°F.

Crust:

   2 cups finely chopped walnuts
   2 tablespoons butter, melted
   2 tablespoons sugar

Combine in Cuisinart and press over bottom and halfway up sides of a 10-inch springform pan.

Filling:

   1 cup sugar
   ¾ cup flour
   ½ cup melted butter
   2 large eggs
   1½ teaspoons Wagner's almond extract
   8 ounces fresh or frozen whole cranberries
   ½ cup coarsely chopped walnuts
   Confectioners' sugar

In a bowl, combine flour and sugar. Reserve. Using the whisk attachment of a mixer, combine butter, eggs and almond extract. Mix in flour and sugar. With a rubber spatula, fold in cranberries and walnuts. Pour into springform pan. Bake in preheated oven for 1 hour and 5 minutes or until the cake is silent. Cool on rack. Sprinkle heavily with confectioners' sugar.

CALVADOS CAKE

Preheat oven to 350°F. Line a 9 × 13 or 11 × 11-inch pan with parchment paper.

 ½ cup calvados or applejack
 4 large apples, peeled, cored and coarsely
     chopped (about 4 cups)
 1 cup chopped walnuts
 1 cup white raisins
 2 cups flour
 ½ cup oil
 2 cups sugar
 2 eggs
 2 teaspoons cinnamon
 1 teaspoon nutmeg
 ½ teaspoon ground cloves
 1 teaspoon salt
 2 teaspoons baking soda

Pour calvados over apples. Mix in walnuts, raisins and flour. In a separate bowl, combine the remaining ingredients and blend thoroughly. Combine with apple mixture. Pour into a parchment paper-lined pan. Bake in the preheated oven for 1 hour or until knife or tester inserted in cake comes out clean. Cool on rack.

CRUMB CAKE

Preheat oven to 375°F. Line a 10 × 12 × 2-inch pan with buttered parchment paper.

   3 cups flour
   1½ cups sugar
   ¼ pound margarine
   ¼ pound butter
   1 teaspoon cinnamon
   ¼ teaspoon nutmeg
   ¼ cup finely chopped Brazil nuts
   2 large eggs
   1 cup milk
   1 teaspoon Grand Marnier
   1 tablespoon baking powder

Combine flour, sugar, margarine and butter in Cuisinart. Reserve 1 cup of crumbs and add cinnamon, nutmeg and nuts to it. Remove remaining dry mixture to mixer and blend in eggs well, one at a time, on the lowest speed of mixer. Add milk, Grand Marnier and baking powder on lowest speed of mixer and combine until well incorporated into batter. Spread batter over bottom of prepared pan. Sprinkle with crumb topping and pat down. Bake in the preheated oven for 45 minutes or until a knife or tester inserted in cake comes out clean. Cool on rack.

TRIPLE CHOCOLATE CAKE

Preheat oven to 350°F. Butter and flour a 10 × 4-inch tube pan.

  1 cup oil
  3 cups sugar
  3 large eggs
  1 tablespoon Wagner's vanilla extract
  6 ounces unsweetened chocolate, melted
  2 cups hot coffee
  3 cups flour
  1 tablespoon baking powder
  ½ teaspoon salt
  1½ cups Maillard's Eagle sweet chocolate or
       Baker's German sweet chocolate, chopped
       to chips in the Cuisinart
  Confectioners' sugar

Beat together the oil and sugar. Add the eggs, one at a time, beating well after each addition. Add vanilla and chocolate. Add coffee and blend thoroughly. Combine flour, baking powder and salt, then incorporate into batter. Fold in chocolate chips. Bake in the preheated oven for 1½ hours, or until knife or tester inserted in cake comes out clean. Cool on rack. Sprinkle with confectioners' sugar.

ORANGE GLAZE CAKE

Preheat oven to 350°F. Butter and flour a 10 × 4-inch tube pan.

Cake:

- ½ cup butter
- ½ cup margarine
- 2 cups sugar
- ½ teaspoon Wagner's vanilla extract
- 5 large eggs
- 3 cups cake flour
- 1 tablespoon baking powder
- ½ teaspoon salt
- ¾ cup milk
- 2 tablespoons grated orange rind
- Confectioners' sugar

Cream shortening, sugar and vanilla in a mixer. Add eggs, one at a time, beating well after each addition. Sift cake flour, baking powder and salt together. Mix flour mixture and milk alternately into batter (⅓ flour, ½ milk, ⅓ flour, ½ milk, ⅓ flour). Fold in rind. Bake in tube pan in the preheated oven for 1 hour and 10 minutes, or until knife or tester inserted comes out clean. Sprinkle with confectioners' sugar.

Glaze:

- ¼ cup butter
- ⅔ cup sugar
- ⅓ cup orange juice

While cake bakes, simmer glaze ingredients for 5 minutes and let cool. When cake is done, cool on rack for 10 minutes. Pour cool glaze over warm cake and let stand for 30 minutes. Turn out and serve.

CHRISTMAS
COOKIES

NOTES ABOUT COOKIES

None of these cookies are difficult to make. They all taste spectacular. They make a perfect Christmas gift for anyone whose taste buds you respect. The problem is that if you don't live alone, they usually don't keep till Christmas, unless you hide them where hungry kids or adults can't find them. The cookies should be stored in tins that have been lined with *wax paper,* not Saran Wrap. The tins should be hidden in the darkest broom closet or attic, where humans rooting around for sweets will never think of looking. My son wouldn't be caught dead in the broom closet lest I suggest he sweep the floor. If your children are more helpful, then they deserve to find the treats.

MINCEMEAT SQUARES

Preheat oven to 350°. Line a 9 × 9-inch pan with buttered parchment paper.

1½ cups regular Quaker Oats
1½ cups flour
1½ cups light brown sugar, firmly packed
½ teaspoon salt
1 teaspoon cinnamon
12 tablespoons sweet butter
1 pound mincemeat (I prefer fresh mincemeat
    which is usually available during the
    holiday season. If canned mincemeat is
    used, add ¼ cup brandy to contents of jar
    and let it sit overnight before using)
½ cup chopped walnuts (2 ounces)

In Cuisinart, combine oats, flour, sugar, salt, cinnamon and butter. Pat ⅔ of mixture in bottom of baking pan. Spread mincemeat over mixture. Combine nuts with remaining oat mixture and sprinkle on top. Bake 40 minutes. Cool. Cut into 1½-inch squares. Makes 3 dozen.

PECAN SANDIES

Preheat oven to 325°F.

½ pound sweet butter
⅓ cup sugar
1 tablespoon water
1 teaspoon Wagner's vanilla extract
2 cups flour
1 cup finely chopped pecans (¼ pound)
Confectioners' sugar (to roll baked cookies in)

In mixer cream butter with sugar. Add water, vanilla, flour and nuts and beat until blended. Roll into finger shapes. Place 1 inch apart on ungreased cookie sheets. Bake for 20 minutes. Remove carefully to rack. When cool, roll in confectioners' sugar. Makes 6 dozen.

WALNUT PUFFS

Preheat oven to 300°F.

½ pound sweet butter
½ cup confectioners' sugar, plus confectioners' sugar to roll puffs in
1 teaspoon Wagner's vanilla extract
2 cups sifted flour
1 cup finely chopped walnuts (¼ pound)

In mixer cream butter. Add ½ cup sugar and vanilla and blend until creamy. Add flour and combine. Add nuts and mix. Roll into balls about 1½ to 2 inches in diameter. Place on ungreased cookie sheet 1 inch apart. Bake for 15 minutes. Roll hot puffs in confectioners' sugar. Let cool on racks. Then roll puffs again in confectioners' sugar. Makes 4 dozen.

MAGIC BARS

Preheat oven to 350°F. Line a 9 × 13-inch baking pan with buttered parchment paper.

    10 tablespoons sweet butter
    2 cups crushed cornflakes
    1 can Eagle sweetened condensed (not
        evaporated) milk
    1 cup miniature chocolate chips
    1 cup grated fresh coconut, or unsweetened
        grated coconut available in health food
        stores
    1 cup finely chopped walnuts (¼ pound)

Melt butter. Mix with cornflakes. Pat mixture evenly over bottom of pan. Drizzle condensed milk evenly over crumbs. Sprinkle on chips, coconut and nuts. Press down gently. Bake for 30 minutes or until golden brown. Cool. Cut into 1½-inch squares. Makes 4 dozen.

CHOCOLATE CHESS SETS

Preheat oven to 325°F.

Dough:

    10 tablespoons sweet butter
    4 ounces cream cheese
    1¼ cups flour

In Cuisinart cut butter, cream cheese and flour together. Blend until ingredients form a ball. Wrap in plastic wrap and chill for 1 hour. Divide into 24 equal portions. With floured fingers press each portion around 1 cup of 2 ungreased 12-cup miniature muffin tins.

Filling:

    2 ounces unsweetened chocolate
    2 tablespoons sweet butter
    ½ cup sugar
    1 large egg
    Pinch of salt
    ½ cup chopped pecans
    1 teaspoon Wagner's vanilla extract
    1 tablespoon brandy
    Whipped cream

Melt chocolate and butter in a double boiler or in microwave oven and remove from heat. Add sugar. In mixer in a separate bowl, lightly beat egg. Add salt, pecans, vanilla and brandy to egg. Add chocolate mixture and mix well.

Fill each crust with an equal amount of filling. Bake 30 minutes. Before serving top with a dab of freshly whipped cream. Makes 2 dozen.

COCO PECAN SQUARES

Preheat oven to 350°F. Butter 9-inch pan.

½ cup butter
½ cup dark brown sugar
1 cup plus 2 tablespoons flour
2 eggs
1 cup light brown sugar
1 cup coarsely chopped pecans
½ cup grated fresh coconut (see
    Magic Bars for form)
1 teaspoon Wagner's vanilla extract
Pinch of salt

In mixer cream butter and dark brown sugar. Add 1 cup flour and blend thoroughly. Press into pan, spreading out into corners. Bake in the preheated oven for 20 minutes.

Beat eggs with light brown sugar until thick. Add pecans. Toss coconut with 2 tablespoons flour and add along with vanilla and salt. Spread topping over crust. Bake for 20 minutes longer. Let cool and cut into squares.

POUND CAKE WAFERS

Preheat oven to 400°F. Butter cookie sheets.

½ pound butter
1 cup sugar
2 large eggs, beaten
2 cups flour
1½ teaspoons nutmeg or mace

In mixer cream the butter and sugar very well. Add eggs. Sift flour and nutmeg several times and add to batter. Drop by teaspoonfuls on cookie sheet. Pat down with the back of a teaspoon that has been dipped in flour. Bake in the preheated oven for about 6 minutes. Cool on rack.

Note:

Do not drop too close together as the cookies spread while baking.

HERMITS

Preheat oven to 325°F. Butter cookie sheets.

½ cup sweet butter
1½ cups sugar
2 eggs
3 cups flour
1 teaspoon cinnamon
1 teaspoon nutmeg
½ cup buttermilk, combined with 1 teaspoon
    baking soda
½ cup pecans, chopped
½ cup dates, cut into small pieces

In a mixer cream butter and sugar until fluffy. Add the eggs, one at a time, beating well after each addition. Sift flour and spices together. Add half the flour, the buttermilk, then the remaining flour, beating until well combined. Mix in dates and nuts. Drop by teaspoonfuls onto cookie sheets. Bake in the preheated oven for 20 minutes. Cool on rack.

Note:

Do not drop too close together because they spread.

VANILLA CHIP COOKIES

Preheat oven to 350°F. Butter cookie sheets.

1 cup butter
⅔ cup sugar
1 large egg
2 teaspoons Wagner's vanilla extract
2½ cups flour
½ teaspoon baking powder
6 ounces white chocolate, chopped in Cuisinart
    into chip-sized pieces

In mixer cream butter and sugar until fluffy. Add egg and vanilla. Sift flour with baking powder and mix in. Add chips by hand. Drop by ½-teaspoonfuls on cookie sheets 2 inches apart. Bake in the preheated oven for 12 minutes. Cool on rack.

PEANUT BUTTER COOKIES

Preheat oven to 350°F. Butter cookie sheets.

1 cup butter
2 cups brown sugar
2 large eggs
1 cup peanut butter
3 cups flour
2 teaspoons baking soda
5 dozen peanut halves

In mixer cream butter and sugar. Add eggs, then peanut butter, beating until well incorporated into batter. Sift flour with baking soda and mix in. Refrigerate until dough may be handled easily, about 1 hour. Roll dough into small balls about 1 inch in diameter. Place on cookie sheets 3 inches apart. Flatten with a fork, once each way to make a crisscross design. Press peanut half into each cookie and bake at 350°F. for 20 minutes. Cool on rack. Makes 5 dozen.

SHORTBREAD COOKIES

Preheat oven to 325°F.

    1 cup sweet butter
    ½ cup confectioners' sugar
    1¾ cups flour
    ¼ teaspoon baking powder

In mixer cream butter and sugar until fluffy. Add flour that has been sifted with baking powder and blend well. Roll out dough to a ¼ to ⅓-inch thickness. Transfer to an ungreased cookie sheet in one piece. Prick all over with a fork. Bake in the preheated oven for 30 minutes, or until lightly brown. Cut into squares after removing from oven. Cool and remove from cookie sheet. Makes about 25 cookies.

IRISH LACE COOKIES

Preheat oven to 350°F. Butter cookie sheets.

  3 eggs
  ¾ teaspoon salt
  1⅓ cups sugar
  1½ tablespoons melted butter
  1 teaspoon Kahlua
  ¼ teaspoon coffee extract
  ¼ teaspoon Wagner's vanilla extract
  ¼ teaspoon grated nutmeg
  4 teaspoons baking powder
  3½ cups uncooked imported Irish quick-cooking
      oatmeal

In mixer beat the eggs well with the salt. Add sugar gradually. Then stir in remaining ingredients on lowest speed of mixer. Drop by teaspoonfuls onto cookie sheets, about a dozen at a time because they tend to spread. Bake in the preheated oven for 10 minutes, or until a delicate brown. Remove from pan at once and place on rack to cool. Makes about 5 dozen.

Optional:

½ cup chopped nuts may be added to the recipe.

PEAR SQUARES

Preheat oven to 350°F.
Line an 8 × 8-inch pan with buttered parchment paper.

> 2 cups dried pears, chopped up finely
>   in Cuisinart
> 1 cup light brown sugar
> 1 cup water
> 1 cup plus 1 tablespoon flour
> 1 teaspoon Wagner's vanilla extract
> 1 teaspoon bicarbonate of soda
> 2 cups cornflakes
> ¾ cup melted butter

Cook pears, ½ cup of the sugar, water and 1 table-spoon of the flour in a saucepan until thick and reserve off heat. Combine the remaining ingredients. Spread ½ of the flour mixture in pan. Cover with pear sauce and spread the rest of the flour mixture on top. Bake in the preheated oven 20 minutes. Cool. Remove from pan and cut into squares. Makes about 2 dozen large or 4 dozen small.

ALVIN'S DELIGHT

Preheat oven to 350°F.
Line an 8 × 8-inch pan with parchment paper.
Crust:

> ½ cup butter
> ½ cup light brown sugar
> 1 cup sifted flour

In mixer cream butter, then add sugar and flour, blend-ing thoroughly. Spread about ¼ inch thick on pan.

Bake at 350°F. for 10 minutes. While baking prepare topping. When baking is done increase oven temperature to 375°F.

Topping:

2 large eggs
½ cup light brown sugar
1 teaspoon Tia Maria
2 tablespoons flour
½ teaspoon baking powder
¼ teaspoon salt
½ cup chopped Brazil nuts
½ cup butterscotch bits
½ cup peanut butter chips
½ cup chopped white chocolate
1 cup grated, fresh coconut (see
    Magic Bars for form)

In mixer beat eggs, then add sugar and Tia Maria and beat until light and fluffy. Sift flour, baking powder and salt together. Add to egg mixture. Add nuts, chips, chocolate and ½ cup of the coconut. Mix thoroughly with egg mixture. Pour over baked crust. Sprinkle with the remaining ½ cup coconut. Bake at 375°F. for 25 minutes, or until topping is firm. Cut into squares when partially cool. These are very rich so small squares are quite adequate. Makes about 5 dozen.

CINNAMON STRIPS

Preheat oven to 350°F.
Butter an 11 × 15 × ¾-inch cookie sheet.

1 cup lightly salted butter
¾ cup sugar
2 cups flour
1 egg, separated
4 teaspoons ground cinnamon
1 teaspoon sherry extract
1 cup chopped pecans
Confectioners' sugar

Cream butter and sugar. Gradually add flour, then egg yolk, cinnamon and extract. Pat down until about ¼ inch thick all over. With a brush spread the unbeaten egg white all over the top, then press chopped pecans down into batter. Bake in the preheated oven for 30 minutes. Cut into oblong pieces when hot. When cool dip in confectioners' sugar. They are delicious in 1-inch × 3-inch fingers. Makes about 3 dozen.

BLONDE BROWNIES

Preheat oven to 325°F.
Line an 8 × 8-inch pan with parchment paper.

2 eggs
1 cup sugar
½ cup lightly salted butter, melted
2 ounces white chocolate, melted in a
    double boiler over simmering water, in a
    pan on a *Flame Tamer* or in a microwave
    oven
¾ cup sifted flour
1 cup finely chopped Brazil nuts
1 teaspoon Tia Maria
¼ teaspoon coffee extract
Confectioners' sugar

In mixer beat eggs slightly, add sugar and stir. Add butter and white chocolate and beat in on lowest speed of mixer. Combine flour and nuts and add to egg mixture. Add Tia Maria and coffee extract, beating until well blended on the lowest speed of the mixer. Pour into pan. Bake in the preheated oven for 35 minutes. Cool and cut into 1-inch × 2-inch fingers. Roll in confectioners' sugar. Makes about 2½ dozen.

FRUITCAKE DROPS

Preheat oven to 300°F. Butter cookie sheets.

2 tablespoons butter
5 tablespoons brown sugar
2 tablespoons ginger marmalade
1 egg
1 teaspoon baking soda
1¾ teaspoons brandy
¾ cup flour
¼ teaspoon allspice
¼ teaspoon ground cloves
¼ teaspoon cinnamon
¼ teaspoon ground nutmeg
2 cups chopped pecans
½ pound golden raisins
¼ pound dried papaya, chopped in Cuisinart
¼ pound dried pineapple, chopped in Cuisinart
¼ pound dried California apricots, chopped in Cuisinart

In mixer cream butter. Add sugar, marmalade and egg, blending thoroughly. Dissolve baking soda in brandy and add to creamed mixture on the lowest setting of mixer. Sift the flour with spices. Gradually add ½ to butter mixture. Dredge nuts and fruits in remaining flour and stir into batter. Mix well. Drop by teaspoonfuls onto cookie sheets. Bake in the preheated oven for 18 minutes. These cookies will ripen like fruitcakes. Makes 5 dozen.

SHORTBREAD SURPRISE

Preheat oven to 325°F.

    4 ounces dried apricots
    2 cups butter
    4 cups flour
    1 teaspoon salt
    ¾ cup confectioners' sugar
    1 teaspoon nutmeg
    1¼ cups grated, fresh coconut (4 ounces)
        (see *Magic Bars* for form)

Chop apricots in Cuisinart and cover with boiling water
for 5 minutes. Drain water and place softened apricots
on paper towels. In mixer cream butter. Beat in flour,
salt, sugar and nutmeg on lowest speed of mixer until
well combined. Place in an ungreased 11 × 15 × ¾-inch
pan and spread around and pat down so batter is about
½ inch thick. Spread apricots over top of batter. Sprinkle coconut over apricots and press into dough. Bake in
the preheated oven for 45 minutes. While hot, cut into
whatever shape you desire.

BRANDY SNAPS

Preheat oven to 350°F.

¼ cup butter
¼ cup sugar
2 tablespoons golden sugar syrup (imported)
½ cup unbleached flour
½ teaspoon pure ginger extract
1 teaspoon Grand Marnier
1 tablespoon grated orange rind
Confectioners' sugar for sprinkling

Cream butter and sugar. Add the remaining ingredients and mix thoroughly but gently. Drop by half-teaspoonfuls on a cookie sheet and bake in the preheated oven for about 7 minutes, or until golden brown. Bake only a dozen at a time as they spread. As soon as you can lift them off the pan, remove them. While they are still warm and pliable, fold each one around your finger so they become shaped like a taco. Sprinkle with confectioners' sugar before serving. If they overcook a little and get a deep brown, don't worry about them. Serve them flat, sprinkled with lots of confectioners' sugar (it hides all the imperfections). Makes about 4 dozen.

DARK RUM BALLS

1½ cups finely ground crumbs from Nabisco
   Famous Wafers
½ cup confectioners' sugar
¾ cup finely ground blanched almonds
1¾ teaspoons cocoa
2 tablespoons light Karo syrup
½ cup Myers's dark rum
Confectioners' sugar for rolling balls

Combine all the ingredients thoroughly and form into small balls. Roll in confectioners' sugar and wrap in aluminum foil to mellow. Makes about 3 dozen.

LUSCIOUS LIME SQUARES

Preheat oven to 350°F. Butter parchment paper to cover bottom and sides of an 8 × 12 × 2-inch pan.

   1 (15-ounce) can sweetened condensed milk
   ½ cup fresh lime juice
   1½ teaspoons grated lime rind
   1½ cups sifted unbleached flour
   1 teaspoon baking powder
   ½ teaspoon salt
   1 teaspoon ground ginger
   11 tablespoons butter
   ¾ cup dark brown sugar, firmly packed
   1 cup uncooked imported oatmeal (quick
      cooking)
   ½ cup finely chopped pecans

Blend together milk, lime juice and rind and set aside. Sift together flour, baking powder, salt and ginger. In mixer cream butter and blend in sugar. Add oatmeal, flour mixture and nuts and beat on lowest speed of mixer until crumbly. Spread about ½ of the flour mixture in the prepared pan and pat down. Spread condensed milk mixture over top of flour mixture and sprinkle remaining crumbs on top of everything. Bake in the preheated oven for about 25 minutes, or until brown around edges. Cool in pan for about 15 minutes at room temperature, refrigerate until firm. Remove from pan and cut into 1¾-inch squares. These cookies should be refrigerated until 1 hour before serving. Makes about 2½ dozen.

THE SUPERJUNK SQUARE

Preheat oven to 325°F. Line an 8 × 8-inch pan with parchment paper.

- ½ cup butter
- ½ cup dark brown sugar
- 1 cup sifted unbleached flour

Combine butter, sugar and flour. Spread about ¼ inch thick on lined pan and bake at 325°F. for 10 minutes. Remove from oven and increase oven temperature to 375°F.

- 2 eggs
- ¾ cups dark brown sugar
- 1 teaspoon Tia Maria
- 2 tablespoons flour
- ½ teaspoon baking powder
- ¼ teaspoon salt
- ¾ cup fresh, grated coconut (see *Magic Bars* for form)
- ½ cup chopped filberts
- ½ cup butterscotch bits
- ½ cup milk chocolate chips
- ½ cup peanut butter chips

Beat eggs, then add sugar and Tia Maria, and beat until light and fluffy. Sift flour, baking powder and salt together. Add ½ cup of the coconut, nuts, bits and chips to flour mixture and combine. Stir in egg mixture and mix thoroughly on low speed of mixer. Spread mixture evenly over top of baked crust and sprinkle with the remaining ¼ cup coconut. Bake at 375°F. for 20 minutes, or until top is firm. Cool. Cut into 1-inch squares while still somewhat warm. These are very rich and sweet. Kids love them.

FLORENTINES

Preheat oven to 350°F. Butter cookie sheets.

¼ cup sugar
¼ cup flour
½ cup heavy cream
¼ cup blanched sliced almonds
¼ cup finely chopped candied orange peel (2
    ounces)
8 to 10 ounces Maillard Eagle sweet chocolate,
    or Baker's German sweet chocolate
1 tablespoon sweet butter

Mix together sugar and flour. Add cream, almonds and candied rind. Drop by teaspoonfuls on cookie sheets about 2 inches apart. Bake for 10 minutes. Remove carefully from sheets and let cool on racks. Melt chocolate and butter in top of double boiler over simmering water or in microwave oven. Spread melted chocolate mixture on flat side of each cooled cookie with a spatula and let harden. Makes 3 to 4 dozen.

TROPICAL TREATS

Preheat oven to 275°F.
Line a 10 × 12 × 2-inch pan with parchment paper.

1 cup sugar
1⅛ teaspoons baking powder
1⅛ cups unbleached flour
½ teaspoon salt
1½ cups dried papaya, chopped fine in Cuisinart
5 tablespoons finely chopped candied ginger
1½ cups chopped pecans
3 eggs, separated
⅛ teaspoon cream of tartar (if egg whites
    are not whipped in copper bowl)
Confectioner's sugar for rolling

Sift together sugar, baking powder, flour and salt. Combine with papaya, ginger and nuts. Beat egg whites and optional cream of tartar with wire whip. Beat egg yolks in separate bowl and stir flour mixture into yolks. Fold in egg whites, using the wire whip of mixer on lowest speed. Press evenly into pan. Bake in the preheated oven for 20 minutes. While hot, cut into 1-inch squares and roll into balls at once (some of the cookie may stick to your hands, and you'll have to rinse them off with hot water from time to time). Roll balls in confectioners' sugar. Makes about 5 dozen.

CHEESECAKE COOKIES

Preheat oven to 350°F.
Line an 8 × 8-inch pan with parchment paper.

   ⅓ cup melted butter
   ⅓ cup light brown sugar, firmly packed
   1 cup unbleached flour
   ½ cup chopped walnuts
   1 (8-ounce) package of cream cheese
   ¼ cup sugar
   1 egg
   1 tablespoon lime juice
   2 tablespoons milk
   1 teaspoon Wagner's almond extract

Mix butter, brown sugar, flour and nuts together in Cuisinart until well combined. Remove 1 cup of mixture and reserve for topping. Place remainder in pan and press down firmly. Bake in the preheated oven for 15 minutes. Beat cream cheese until smooth with sugar. Add egg, lime juice, milk and almond extract. Pour onto the baked crust, top with reserved crumbs and return to oven for 25 minutes longer. Cool thoroughly in refrigerator and then cut into squares. These cookies should be refrigerated until an hour before serving.

COCONUT KISSES

Preheat oven to 300°F. Butter cookie sheets.

> ¾ cup sweetened condensed milk
> ½ pound shredded fresh coconut (see
>   *Magic Bars* for form)
> ½ teaspoon pineapple extract
> 1 cup chopped Brazil nuts
> ¼ cup chopped white chocolate

Combine all the ingredients and drop by teaspoonfuls onto a well-buttered cookie sheet. Bake in the preheated oven for 12 minutes. Cool on racks.

WALNUT FINGERS

Preheat oven to 275°F. Line a 10 × 15 × ¾-inch pan with buttered parchment paper.

> 6 egg whites
> ⅛ teaspoon cream of tartar (if egg whites
>   are not whipped in a copper bowl)
> 2 cups cake flour, sifted
> ⅛ teaspoon salt
> 1 teaspoon baking powder
> 1 pound brown sugar, sifted
> 3 cups chopped walnuts
> 1 tablespoon Drambuie

Beat egg whites until they begin to foam, by using the wire whip of the mixer at the highest speed, and adding cream of tartar (if whites are not whipped in copper bowl). Stop when the whites stand up in peaks. Sift flour, salt and baking powder together. Add brown sugar and mix until combined. Reserve ½ cup of the mixture and dredge walnuts in it. Fold in the rest into the egg whites on lowest speed of mixer with wire whip. Fold in walnuts dredged in flour and Drambuie. Spread over pan. Bake in the preheated oven for 60 minutes. When cool cut into fingers.

BLACK WALNUT BRANDY BROWNIES

Preheat oven to 325°F. Line a 10 × 15 × ¾-inch baking pan with buttered parchment paper.

    1 pound black walnuts, chopped
    8 ounces unsweetened chocolate
    ½ pound sweet butter
    8 eggs
    ½ teaspoon salt
    4½ cups sugar
    1 teaspoon vanilla
    ¼ cup brandy
    2 cups flour
    Confectioners' sugar for sprinkling

Toast black walnuts and set aside. Melt chocolate and butter in top of double boiler over simmering water or in microwave oven. Set aside. In mixer beat eggs until fluffy. Add salt, sugar, vanilla, brandy and blend. Add chocolate mixture, flour and toasted nuts. Mix. Spread in pan and bake for 45 minutes. Let cool. Cut into 1½-inch squares. Sprinkle with confectioners' sugar. Makes 5 dozen.

DROP SAND TARTS

Preheat oven to 375°F. Butter a cookie sheet.

¼ pound sweet butter
1 cup sugar
2 large eggs
1¼ cups sifted flour
1 teaspoon baking powder
Freshly grated nutmeg
Finely chopped nuts (optional)

Cream butter and sugar. Add 1 egg. Combine flour and baking powder. Add to batter and mix well. Drop by ½-teaspoonfuls on cookie sheet 2 inches apart. Beat remaining egg. Flatten cookies very thin with fork dipped into beaten egg. Sprinkle with sugar and nutmeg. May also be sprinkled with finely chopped nuts. Bake 10 to 12 minutes. Remove from cookie sheet and cool on racks. Makes 6 to 7 dozen.

CARMELITAS

Preheat oven to 350°F. Line a 9 × 9-inch pan with buttered parchment paper.

1½ cups flour
1½ cups regular Quaker Oats
1 cup light brown sugar, firmly packed
¾ teaspoon baking soda
Pinch of salt
¼ pound sweet butter
1 cup miniature chocolate chips
½ cup chopped walnuts
2 envelopes Ancel caramel (or 4 tablespoons
    caramel topping)

In Cuisinart or by hand combine flour, oats, sugar, soda, salt and butter until mixture is the texture of cornmeal. Press ½ of mixture over bottom of pan. Bake for 10 minutes. Sprinkle chips, walnuts and caramel over baked base. Press remaining oat mixture on top and bake for 25 minutes longer. Cool and cut into 1½-inch squares. Makes 3 dozen.

BOURBON BALLS

¼ cup cocoa plus cocoa for rolling cookies in
3 cups crushed vanilla wafers (1 box)
1 cup confectioners' sugar
1 cup finely chopped walnuts (¼ pound)
¼ cup Karo light corn syrup
⅓ cup bourbon

Combine cocoa, crumbs, sugar and nuts. Add corn syrup and bourbon. Let stand for 30 minutes. Pinch off bits the size of a walnut and roll into balls. Roll in cocoa. Wrap in colored aluminum foil. Age for at least two weeks before eating. Makes 50 to 60.

CHRISTMAS BONUS
GEORGIA MOON EGG NOG

8 large eggs
¾ teaspoon salt
1 cup sugar
1 cup Georgia Moon corn liquor or bourbon
½ cup Myers's rum
1 quart heavy cream

Beat eggs until foamy. Add salt, sugar and liquors. Mix together. In a separate bowl, lightly whip cream. Fold everything together and let season in refrigerator for a day or two. Stir and serve in stem goblets with fresh nutmeg grated on top. Serves 12 to 16.

KITCHEN POWER!

☐	20480	**COMPLETE CONVECTION OVEN COOKBOOK** J. Scott	$2.9
☐	01281	**COOK'S TOOLS** Susan Campbell	$9.95
☐	20015	**COOKING WITH HERBS AND SPICES** Craig Claiborne	$3.50
☐	20602	**SOURDOUGH COOKERY** Rita Davenport	$2.95
☐	20427	**MASTERING MICROWAVE COOKING** Scotts	$2.75
☐	20954	**PUTTING FOOD BY** Hertzberg, Vaughan & Greene	$3.95
☐	22565	**LAUREL'S KITCHEN** Robertson, Flinders & Godfrey	$4.95
☐	20995	**CROCKERY COOKERY** Mable Hoffman	$2.95
☐	13168	**THE COMPLETE BOOK OF PASTA** Jack Denton Scott	$2.25
☐	20661	**MADAME WU'S ART OF CHINESE COOKING**	$2.95
☐	13731	**BETTER HOMES & GARDENS ALL-TIME FAVORITE CASSEROLES**	$2.50
☐	20050	**THE CHICKEN AND THE EGG COOKBOOK** M. L. Scott & J. D. Scott	$3.95
☐	14866	**BETTER HOMES & GARDENS NEW COOKBOOK**	$3.95
☐	20242	**BETTY CROCKER'S COOKBOOK**	$3.50
☐	20583	**THE ART OF JEWISH COOKING** Jennie Grossinger	$2.50
☐	14943	**MAKE-A-MIX COOKING** Scotts	$2.75
☐	01326	**OLD-FASHIONED RECIPE BOOK** Carla Emery	$12.95
☐	20223	**MICROWAVE COOKERY** Deacon	$2.95

Buy them wherever Bantam Bestsellers are sold or use this handy coupon:

Bantam Books, Inc., Dept. KP, 414 East Golf Road, Des Plaines, Ill. 60016

Please send me the books I have checked above. I am enclosing $_____ (please add $1.00 to cover postage and handling). Send check or money order —no cash or C.O.D.'s please.

Mr/Mrs/Miss _____

Address _____

City _____ State/Zip _____

KP—5/82

Please allow four to six weeks for delivery. This offer expires 11/82.

<u>SAVE $2.00</u> ON YOUR NEXT BOOK ORDER!

BANTAM BOOKS ❦

Shop-at-Home
Catalog

Now you can have a complete, up-to-date catalog of Bantam's inventory of over 1,600 titles—including hard-to-find books.

And, you can <u>save $2.00</u> on your next order by taking advantage of the money-saving coupon you'll find in this illustrated catalog. Choose from fiction and non-fiction titles, including mysteries, historical novels, westerns, cookbooks, romances, biographies, family living, health, and more. You'll find a description of most titles. Arranged by categories, the catalog makes it easy to find your favorite books and authors and to discover new ones.

So don't delay—send for this shop-at-home catalog and save money on your next book order.

Just send us your name and address and 50¢ to defray postage and handling costs.